WITHOUT HER

WITHOUT HER

MEMOIR OF A FAMILY

PATSY CREEDY

atmosphere press

BODIES

They wanted. They didn't even know it as such, but they wanted. They pretended to bang the ends of their forks on the table, saw their chunky silver knives against the wrinkled silver edges of their TV dinners. They were always hungry. They wanted more mass, more volume, more heat. They turned the broken knob on the TV, yanking the wrench that served to change the channel from each other, cranking it and the volume till their ears ached with its sound and with a creeping fear and its coming silence accompanying the return of their father, tires crunching up the driveway.

They wanted music on the radio, more of it—not droning gray news. They wanted guitar solos, yowling lyrics of the pain they couldn't name. They wanted muscles in their skinny arms. They had tiny rodent bones, easily digested by reptiles; they wanted hard white skeletal mass. They were wolves, five left over pups whose fur was much too soft, yet they could transform themselves when they willed it into a thieving animal body, taking fruit from the fields, food from the stores, cars from the street.

When it was cold, they fought for a place on the couch,

fighting for possession of their father's green army blanket of itchy wool. When it got damp and cold, when the rain fell and they were soaked from splashing home through all of the growing puddles, the middle one would crawl onto the couch, curling under the blanket with the oldest or the youngest, whoever was cold enough to receive him without attack.

When they fought, they fought with dirt clods, with dishtowels wetted at the end, with vacuum hoses, with angry yanks as they pulled down the mattresses from each other's beds, toppling them down onto the floor, the mattresses sliding down onto mounds of dirty clothes, crumbs from the seams of the bedding flying into the air like sugary dust. They grabbed whatever was nearest and would cause the most harm: a favorite doll, a transistor radio, a wobbly bookshelf—they wanted it all to crash and be loudly destroyed.

And when their dad came home from work or from one of his long solitary drives, they would hide in their destroyed bedrooms, hoping he was too tired to wonder where they were. "Buckaflap" the middle brother had named their father, short for 'bucket of flab'—a code name created for ridiculing how large he was, how fat and slovenly, his giant belly round and firm like a Michelin man in the large khaki pants he bought twice a year at Alder's Big and Tall Shop in Berkeley.

They sometimes got the belt for the destruction they'd caused. They never saw each other's injuries, they never looked, except the two girls, changing at night into their flannel nightgowns, the pink rosettes brushing over their marked skin. The belt never drew blood, just red welts that looked like stencils across their backs, red shapes of hidden meaning trailing across the backs of their tiny legs. They didn't understand the something on the other side of the pain, the welting stain of frustration and crushing sadness coming from their father's wrists when he hit them. Maybe there was some kind of message Buckaflap was trying to send to them, awakening them to his world, the adult world laced with the disappointment and pain he drew with each breath, transmitting this onto their raised soft skin, tattooing his anger, man anger, anger like a building falling, its dry cloudy dust rushing out into the air with each blow.

And when their father was gone, they wanted to be like him, to master the power they saw in an invisible halo, threatening in its light ringing around the outline of his body. They hunted, scattering and threatening imaginary animals in the fields attached to their back yard. They walked single file through the tall bright green grasses of spring. They found tiny birds, crept into neighboring yards, stole fruit from the thickening trees. They counted on their father being too tired to ask where they had been at the end of the long days of summer. They relied on his defeat.

But there were times when they were a body at rest, summer mornings when he was gone to work and they had had enough cereal and milk and there were cartoons on one of the few channels on their black and white TV. In those moments they let the oldest one be the father, the benevolent man boss who was willing to take them in, to give them this momentary peace. Those warm mornings they let themselves be worn out. They breathed quietly, their skinny rib cages barely rising with the tiny movement. They were silent then, not wanting, not grasping, just children watching cartoons, tracing the design in the carpet with a finger; no thoughts, just light.

ARCHIPELAGO

The five of them became a chain of tiny islands after her death. They were continental fragments, their bodies floating in the shadow of the land mass they had come from, broken off from their mother's mainland when she died that spring afternoon, just six weeks after the youngest girl was born. Their mother's body was their lost center, their magma, what was left of their destroyed volcanic heart.

They were a stunned animal body, witness to her disappearance, magnified in their bones that day. Her lost life an atoll detonated, no protective goggles provided for the spectacle, the mushroom cloud of her death sealing their sky. The negative space filling their tiny atmosphere with a new emptiness. Her death left nothing of their former landscape behind, no familiar buildings, no trees, no insects, all beasts particulated in the heavy heaving air of her death. The lacquered lagoons of their islands inverted and tossed into the sky, thrown angrily back down to earth, as ever changed droplets of liquid hot matter, forever altered in their landing.

Their remaining shape stayed rooted under water, its

darkened edges like a penciled tracing of what used to be, bones of a destroyed land, their watery base an archeology when viewed from above, a scattered skeletal frame still able to discern the proof of her original mountain.

They knew they were *Of Her*. They pulled in close in a ragged reformation that followed her death. Each child a lonely nameless island in their shared faraway sea chain, their tectonic, motherless displacement shifting further and further away from her memory as the years went by, a widening separateness evolving, time sliding away any adjacent continent, isolation the air they learned to breath best.

When they were small, the questions they held about her death remained in the strange trees of their new world like shiny island leaves. They knew the answers they wanted were not possible and to ask was to invite the dark. Their father was the captain of their new land mass, working hard to steer their course, lost in the remaining light, trying to rebuild their world back into its original shape because he knew no other—could imagine no other—without her. He didn't realize he was the ship while they had become land, originating from her earth, that they now existed as their own entity, a diffuse country of hidden channels, links of blood, conduits of mother born necessity their father didn't possess, couldn't comprehend even if he wanted to.

He tried to gather the things he remembered, to make a diorama of their old life, a replica, inserting a new figure of a woman, in the shape of a mother, to represent all she had been to them. Once he even tried a stepmother, then a revolving door of housekeepers, continually replacing them on their island out cropping. The five of them watched, waiting to see what or who was going to be dropped into their still life next. They dispassionately watched the women, the housekeepers, those who stayed and those who left, those who tried to make order out of pity, vacuuming the dead cells and hair from the bare wood floors of their mother's house. They knew not to care about them.

They resided in the papery structure, the daily lid of silence belying the jagged newly formed land they were becoming, a hardening land where arriving animals frequently died quickly. They were an island chain, the memory of their mother lodged in their bodies, laced tiny islands existing in a jet stream, air flowing over their mountain crater, the origin and the echo of their mother. Their collective memory of grief could cause the wind to rise, quickly pulling in a blinding fog hiding the torturous cliffs, one child peak calling to another in the craterous ring of fire.

As her children they guarded the imperceptible, imagined shape of her body, recreating her face, her teeth, the color of her hair, like four tiny white-haired warriors, the middle boy's hair dark brown just like hers, fearful that if they didn't remain vigilant she would disappear even more. There was no word for how her absence shattered their bones, loss thrown into the fragmented ecology of their sunbaked bodies, the broken mantle of her essence was where they wanted to reside, but it no longer existed, her memory a necessary place to land, the sea washing up to its shore, only to inevitably roll back, leaving them without her still and always stomping forth in their tiny bodies.

They stayed close in the beginning, when they were

kids, a pack of children adrift, a ball of churning legs and arms, matted hair and bloodied knees, their loyalty to their roiling form the only thing that mattered, their father a grown up to be appeased and avoided, his reach unpredictable and often painful. They could see no map of their shared history with him even though everyone told them he was their father. He was an essential part of their history, yet they could not perceive him as anything other than a father object, a grown up, *their* grown up, meant to do certain things. They had no design to comprehend their cellular connection, embodied beneath their dirty fingernails, in the angle of their matching high foreheads and long legs, their minds not ready, their bodies mere chrysalises folded in shiny waiting, unable to know the pain that held their father captive, blinded, a primate batting blindly at anything and everything coming at him at the entrance to his own dark cave of grief.

They learned to look innocent, experts of the deadpan face, no eye contact, just keep moving. Each of their lonely island currents touched without words below their sea, the slender land bridges between them microscopically eroding in the night dreams they once shared as children, glinting grains trickling undetected, slipping away incrementally night after night, moving their aftermath lives into silvery memory flattened like wings of a dead sea bird, a gull maybe, the hot sun unfettered and burning, just getting on with the monstrous, each new moment enormous as space.

ANIMALS

Their father had always loved animals. He once built a rabbit hutch in a corner of their backyard, a half-acre of a sub-divided fallow farmer's field, choked with tall green weeds in the springtime. He placed perfectly measured hooks on the wood framed doors and lined the bottom with wire to keep the rabbits enclosed, but small enough that their padded feet did not get stuck. The hutch had a one-sided slanted roof and looked like a perfectly made example from a wood shop class or some arts and craft summer camp sample never to be recreated. Its promised simplicity was a little sinister, being from the foreign world of adults who were always saying how easy everything would be to do when they knew it would be a mess in their small hands.

It sat empty a year later. A lost dog or some other kind of animal got into the hutch one night, killing all five of the rabbits, one for each of them. That Sunday morning, when their father found the carnage, he warned them as they watched cartoons not to go outside and vanished out the back door. They did not bother to get up from their bellies where they were gathered watching TV, only looked at each other and then back at the screen. It was one of the few times he tried to keep the many small violences of their childhood from them.

They could never talk their father into a dog though, the solid *No* resounding from him a constant, like a cough. He only allowed caged pets—snakes, turtles, and many fish tanks of shiny fish. The two girls used to try to catch the pet store fish sleeping in their tank when they walked by them on the way to the bathroom in the middle of the night. They held hands and scuttled quickly on the cold wood floor, trying to reach the bathroom before the unnamed beings of the dark grabbed their feet or the edge of their nightgowns. The fish tank was a landmark, its light a beacon taking them to safety. The Neon Tetras and the large silver Angelfish ever wide-eyed and always moving, their algae-covered tank lit up like a lone gas station in the dark.

None of them knew until much later about the dogs their father and mother raised in the early years of their marriage. They felt betrayed and then sad for their father when they found out, the dogs being part of the blank that was their parents' history before they had them. Their parents had raised German Shepherds in their backyard for several years when they lived in Daly City. The constant gloom of fog coming off the ocean was a good climate for the dogs. They were a furry breed and didn't do well in the heat. The dogs and their pups took over the backyard, their exploration and digging covering every square inch of the yard with a gray brown dust. Their pawing destroyed every green thing that poked up from the earth.

It was hard to imagine their father and mother before

they were born, it was especially hard to imagine their mother being or doing anything but being gone, the missing piece to their lives. They collectively decided to place this discovery about the dogs into their tomb of unspoken things, a secret to be shared like a somber gift, like a small but important find from an archeological dig that frequently yielded nothing. They knew from past experience they could not predict how their father might react when they mentioned anything to do with their mother. Sometimes he was silent, as though he didn't hear them. Sometimes he blew up, yelling at them to stop asking some many questions.

Their father held the memories of their mother and of his life with her before they were born deep in his body, unwilling or unable to share her with them. The wall of grief he built was a solid untouchable place, yet its careful geometry was still sometimes a little porous, allowing some movement, some memory to travel across its lattice like a floating seed. He could still sometimes feel the current of fresh pain, its far-off threat lurking, a faint air raid siren coming through his lungs, souring his belly when he had to talk about her. He froze her and the pain she left in him like a stone, like an imbedded object—a bullet, a splinter of glass stuck in place—scar tissue fusing and blurring over the enormous shape of his loss.

Their father sometimes varied his one syllable answers about getting a dog from *No* to *Nope* or a merely silent shake of his Bryll-creamed head. The Bryll Cream was a strange hair grease he used religiously to tame his graying curls. It was the only hint of vanity or grooming in an otherwise bland bar soap hygiene routine. The cream smelled terrible, like industrial garage sadness, as did the

Lava soap, often the only soap found in the bathroom sink. The Lava was rough and often smeared with the greasy gray shades of a life that needed another agent to get through it all, to reach the raw skin underneath the mess.

They knew not to argue when he said no, but to retreat, to regroup when necessary. They knew they needed to find another angle to get what they wanted from him. Even the middle boy, who came to earth with a different type of mind, one wired with risk and fearless curiosity. His was a mind unafraid of pain, even he understood the wisdom of retreat at a certain kind of *no*. The middle brother usually chose to circumvent their father, do what he couldn't help but do, and frequently got caught. Don't ask, play dumb and apologize later would become his well-worn strategy.

They eventually tricked their father into their first dog, Jacob. The youngest brother, who became their father's teenaged task master was the one who came up with the plan that finally worked. The others called him the little wife behind his back. He went to the grocery store for their dad when he could drive, he filled the Volkswagen van with gas and kept an eye on the younger girls, notifying their father when the oldest got home late or locking her out so she had to silently climb through a window, scraping her legs as she slid inside, hoping not to wake their father.

This youngest brother, who now had a certain status with Buckaflap, came up with the idea to tell Buckaflap that he had been asked to dog sit a dog for a week, and would that be okay? One week turned into two and by then their father was in love, smiling freely at the dog and scratching his ears, talking to him in a sweet voice they had never heard him use before. When their father asked, the youngest brother freely admitted the scheme.

BARN

They lived in an old farmhouse with a faded white barn at the end of a gravel driveway. They moved there sometime after their father divorced Charlene, their momentary stepmother. The farmhouse was rundown and needed a lot work before they could move in, but it had four bedrooms and a small detached cottage. The half-acre of weed-choked earth they acquired with the house was all that remained of someone's farm life. The gravel driveway filled with many tiny rivulets of rain in the rainy months, their muddy footprints rerouting some of the little waterways into murky boot shaped pools as they ran for shelter or splashed for sport, the goal often to hit every puddle they could on the way to the backdoor.

The backyard fences of the neighboring houses bordered their square of weed-covered land. There was a vacant lot directly behind the old barn, full of high wet grass in the springtime. They soaked their pants and sneakers as they traversed the field, hands gliding across the tops of the weeds, wading through them like bright green water. An old willow tree sat on one edge of the lot, its thin long branches uninteresting to them as they made poor weapons and were inedible so therefore of no value, disappearing into mere landscape in their daily outside dramas.

At the other corner of the vacant lot was a tall wooden fence that hid a pool, the crown jewel of any childhood neighborhood, its value supreme. The freedom and relief in the cool bright blue water, an almost spiritual quenching in the long hot summers. The mother in the house with the pool would let them swim there sometimes but would rarely let even the two younger sisters inside her house, fearing their wild would get on the furniture or into her children.

The little girl who lived in the house behind the fence with the pool was cunning and needy. Her sister and brother were much older than her and doing shining things in high school and college. They stepped past her on their way to the bathroom, slamming their bedroom doors as she trailed after them in the hall, telling them of the small awful things she had learned about someone in the neighborhood, usually one of the three brothers in the house with the scrappy white barn.

The needy girl with the pool ate any candy and cookies she received with tiny rodent-like bites, meticulously sucking on a piece of hard candy until it was small and wafer thin, flaunting what was left with her mouth open, showing the two sisters when they played with her. The older sister watching the needy girl with closed eyes when she did this, wanted to snatch the shiny translucency out of her mouth and throw it on the ground or pop it into her own hungry mouth and crush it.

She knew about hunger in a hollowed belly sense. She was hungry from being fed a steady diet of cold cereal and

Instant Breakfast mixed with powered milk for breakfast and dinners of Tuna Casserole or Hamburger Helper. Any ice cream or cookies their father brought home from the grocery store would quickly vanish, usually into the middle brother's possession the moment their father put them in the kitchen cupboard, the middle brother always unseen and faster than the rest of them.

The contents of the barn consisted of mostly of cast-off things they didn't want in their bedrooms anymore. There were scattered cardboard boxes drooping into soft mounds, stray tools and bulging brown paper bags full of old school work and cast-off clothing, abandoned on the floor of the barn like a town of small paper encampments.

Then there were their bicycles of strictly delineated ownership, the younger ones knowing never to even attempt to ride the oldest brother's green ten speed under the threat of being tortured on the living room carpet, face down, not being allowed to move until he said so. Anything they no longer valued was tossed in the barn, forgotten as it landed, abandoned to the mice and spiders. Sometimes one of them would get the urge to rummage in the boxes and bags, hoping for forgotten treasure on a dull afternoon. They hoped to find lost money or maybe a trace of their mother in a book or a forgotten photo.

The back of the barn had a high window, a square of midday light coming through the dimness of the barn. Occasionally errant brown birds flew in and quickly flew back out. It was pretty easy to climb up the exposed wood frame to reach the rafters, and the edge of the window, which made a perfect seat to look out over the backyard and the neighboring houses. This was often the middle brother's roost. He would sit there, sometimes boldly smoking a cigarette when their father was gone, sometimes just sitting, not moving or talking, a quiet state that was unusual and felt dangerous to the younger siblings who left him alone, trying to stay out of his line of site as they walked past the back of the barn.

The barn burned down one summer. To say something burned down always seems to imply that whatever caught fire literally burned to the ground, no structure left, only smoking black charcoal chunks. But what it really meant was that the remaining building was now a half charred skeleton, any walls or other structure left partially standing, the ceiling caved in and gaping, the roof now lost to the sky framed in singed edges. It meant uninhabitable and ruined but still unfinished, a wooden corpse demanding its evidence be vanquished, its useless remains in need of a burial.

The two little sisters were attending the summer program at their elementary school that morning, making potholders for an imaginary mother out of strange loops of stretchy fabric. Their bellies full from the free meal provided, peanut butter and jelly sandwiches and a carton of cold, real milk. After the program ended at noon they went to the Stantons' house and were having a snack (more food) around the shiny polished wood dining room table when the phone rang.

The middle brother was there at the table with them that day, which was a little strange but not too strange as he often roamed the neighborhood with the two Stanton boys. The three of them formed an edgy, snake-mean body—their groupthink capable of many a neighborhood theft or some kind of vandalism.

Mrs. Stanton was a soft warm woman, her life a rolling

spool of iridescent thread unraveling out to her children. The thread emitting from her dimming and trailing underneath the table when her husband came home, the atmosphere in the house changing like a switch plate over into the frequency of his male orbit. She was one of the few mothers in the neighborhood who allowed them to play with her children and actually let them into her house. She smiled and called them by name, and looked directly at them when she asked them if they would like a snack or a drink of water.

The older girl and Laura Stanton would sometimes play car, sitting in the giant old green Chevrolet kept in the garage, a treasured possession of the Stanton father. The steering wheel was huge and pastel green with knuckled grips, wide like a shield, their little arms stretched out straight as they pretended to drive, yelling at imaginary children in the back seat, surviving horrible accidents and swearing quietly at other drivers so Laura's mother could not hear the insults and end the game if they couldn't be nice. Laura Stanton was a little wily too. She wished she could steal and break windows and fight the other kids at school like her brothers did. She wanted something, anything to happen outside the small scope of school and church and inside voices.

What happened that day after the phone call about the barn or who even called to tell them about the fire is a blank. There was the eerie sense that day in their comingled sibling body that the middle brother could easily have done this, immediately followed by the ill-fitting but comforting fact that he was with them when they found out, so how could he have started the fire? They chose to believe that he was not guilty in this particular incident, the physical evidence of him at the table with them at the Stanton's the resting point of their desired truth for their brother.

Later that afternoon their father flew up the driveway in the Volkswagen van, quickly getting out and pulling each child to him, hugging one and then moving onto the next one, counting them with his touch. Not much else is clear about that day. Their father's strange tenderness was out of character and never spoken of again, but remembered by them all. It was a strange artifact in their childhood and the smallest glimmer of softness.

LUPOI'S

They swam like nut colored otters, sliding in and out of the clear chlorinated water of the neighborhood pool, one with the other children that summer. They did things like other children, children with a father and mother and cupboards full of food in bright cellophane packages soon to be filling their bellies. They were simply children then, summer time at the pool in drooping wet shorts or a hand me down one piece, followed later by tiny bikinis, too large or too small, barely covering what parents knew and feared, sex dormant like a bulb in their earth. During that summer before the fire, they were just children splashing and yelling, trying for a giant splash as they jumped into the pool, dripping clear ribbons of water onto the hot concrete when they pulled themselves out of the pool.

The youngest brother was silent most of the time. He frequently sat unmoving for long periods of time watching TV on the couch while the two older brothers discussed the merits of certain cars or movies or parts of girl's bodies, the youngest brother would sometimes suddenly erupt with some odd fact on point to whatever their argument was. This usually stunned the two older brothers into a momentary silence, hopefully followed by fits of laughter instead of a punch in the arm, knuckle to the bone, the correct form for a direct hit.

These outbursts from the youngest brother came forth from a small vent in his psyche, steam escaping from the watcher he knew he was, burdened and occasionally liberated by human speech, silence was a necessity for him, for his way of being, like his eye color or height. He was quiet at school during recess before he became the candy king, then later he often got in trouble for talking too much in class, again the eruptions of comic spot-on facts or clever puns sending the class into gales of laughter, leaving the teacher steaming at her bad luck at having one of the five motherless siblings in her class.

The youngest brother was large, square from the back, his stomach smooth and pale, hanging down like a giant fruit fed on a sugary midnight formula found inside the many yellow and orange candy wrappers, lying like forgotten leaves under his bed, their contents quickly swallowed. The endless need for more candy a desire spreading itself silently, fueled each afternoon as they filed into Lupoi's Market, walking slowly, leisurely like they imagined adults might do. In the store they spread out like a spill. The two girls sometimes leaning their small bodies on the slanted cool glass of the meat case, looking and pointing at the chicken feet or the giant cow tongue laying like a corpse between inch high ruffles of green plastic.

The youngest brother always wore gigantic clothes, his tee shirt and jacket hanging on his towering frame. He had the strange ability some people have to be able to disappear in plain sight. In a group he was able to fade and morph into an invisible energy the mind had trouble holding onto, even with his large frame. He used this ability to his advantage, that and playing the clown. Many people thought he was simple, a lost boy from that poor family, left to fend for himself in the wake of his mother's tragic death. He could feel the pity like a fine mist, and it made him want to take more and harder.

They were all thieves, the two older brothers more inclined to bigger stakes, robbing houses and stores and stealing cars, but the youngest brother was the best candy thief in the family. He looked like just any other awkward blond pre-teen boy, his eyes wide and blue behind his greasy glasses. He moved slick and silent as he methodically filled his pockets with loot. He soon became the candy king, kids at school running up to him wanting to buy the long dusty ropes of gum, the bright SweeTarts and shiny Hot Tamales, whatever he had that day. He was a dealer of his first addiction, candy, and of being wanted by the crowd.

The girls weren't expected to steal candy, they just had to be quiet and distracting to grown ups if need be. They learned how to steal later on when their brother became less generous and wanted to charge them for his product. The sisters roamed around the store, pointing with disgust at the thick fat rim circling the New York steaks, gasping at the impossible height of the filet mignons, which they called *mig-nons*. They were sure such parts of those beasts would never cook all the way through, imagining with disgust the bloody thing landing on one of their plates, raw and dead looking on the inside. They were horrified at the idea of having to attempt to eat that huge hunk of steak, their tiny stomachs yearning only for sugar at every opportunity, candy their currency, their comfort, their first escape.

It is unclear who discovered Lupoi's as their ready cache of candy revenue. The oldest brother claimed he found it but the youngest brother, with the growing belly hanging over the top of his jeans perfected the technique. There were two entrances to Lupoi's even though it was a small market. The candy aisle was near the back entrance, the rows of candy spread out like an accordion, like a flexed wing of a giant tropical bird, tidy and intricate with color. The Lifesavers and gum and breath mints were at the top of the strata, followed by the mid-size chocolate bars, the Snickers, the Milky Ways, the Butterfingers. Then there were the rows of the smaller penny candies, Fireballs, Pez and Abazabas, Butter Mints and salt-water taffy, its opaque pastel wrappers quieter to the touch in their waxy paper.

There was a mirror high up in one of the corners of the store, a large fixed eyeball to watch for shoplifters. The youngest brother discovered it early on and was usually careful to avoid its eye as he filled his pockets. The girls never saw him actually steal anything, even though they wanted to, but they witnessed with greedy glee the pile of loot he pulled out from the invisible bulk of his clothing when they got home.

While the two sisters were waiting for their brother to signal them he was ready to go, they gazed blandly at a pineapple tower in the produce section, wondering how sharp the leaves really might be, daring each other to touch one of the tips. Mr. Lupoi's son appeared and grabbed them both by their stick like arms, walking them briskly to the front of the store where they saw the youngest brother standing wedged into a corner near the cash register. The middle brother had bolted out the back door as he already had a probation officer so it was understood by all of them that he couldn't get into any more trouble with the police.

On the counter by the cash register was a large pile of candy and gum. The girls were impressed with this particular haul and forgot for a brief moment that they were in big trouble, their eyes widening at the array. As they were looking at the candy and looking at their brother for some kind of a sign as to what to do next, a police car pulled up and two officers got out of the patrol car and headed briskly into the store. Their brother's face was completely closed down, no flicker of recognition in his eyes to tell them what to do.

The three of them were taken to the police station in the back of the police car, the two girls sitting close to each other, their legs touching. They were all silent, the girls watching their brother carefully, who did not utter a word. The policemen forgot themselves for a minute and made a few jokes about their brother's proficiency as a shoplifter, then remembered and scolded them the rest of the way to the police station.

When they got to the police station the two policemen in the car took the youngest brother into a room and closed the door. The two girls were left sitting on a long shiny oak bench, their legs swinging back and forth, not touching the floor. They waited on the bench, trying to see if they could touch the back of the wall with their shoes if they swung their legs hard enough.

NIGHT BIRDS

The middle brother was the one who put the live cat in their neighbor's mailbox—cruelly squeezing the poor animal into the oversized white painted mailbox—just to scare the neighbors when they went to get the mail a few hours later, no other reason, no grudge, just an impulse that had to been followed, burning in his brain.

No one was watching in the silence of the summer morning, mothers slowly stirring in their robes, too soon in the day to look out the window into the stillness, the unchanging green life they found themselves in for another stultifying day. No one saw him struggling with the cat and the mailbox. Rural life and the invisibility of children was something he capitalized on, sometimes very capable of delayed gratification.

The night they stole the baby ducks became a shared saga of their childhood, all of them owning it. It became funny and sweet in the re-telling, a harmless antic of their youth. In hindsight it was a small crime in the measure of those to come. The middle boy had discovered some baby ducks in his bored wanderings along the hot asphalt roads, stick in hand, slicing the air as he swung at buckeyes, which mostly thudded into the dirt, no fight in them.

They lived near the end of the suburban limits, the full summer trees leaning over the roads, hiding the older houses, the silent trees there long before the land was subdivided. The road at the end of the neighborhood doubled back on itself, forking into newer cul-de-sacs where the trees thinned out into young nothings, held up with wooden poles and bits of wire. The other fork in the road turned towards town, following a tiny creek, occasional hand hewn wooden or cement bridges leading the way to the houses hidden in the trees. In summer the numerous fruit trees fed all the children living in the neighborhood; peaches and nectarines and small sour apples, and the regal pomegranates, the favorite, the prize to be plucked from the unsuspecting houses. The pomegranate's seed clusters stained their fingernails and skin, stained their clothes with the blood dark seeds, juicy nests of shiny red seeds orderly and gleaming once you got through the thick yellowed skin.

It was on one of those endless summer days of boredom, a day pushing down on them with a sharp longing for some unnamed thing, an *any*thing to happen. It was a sense that there must be an imagined hidden life that others are living, untouchable to them as children in the hot yellow sun. The middle brother had the idea to steal the baby ducklings he had found in his wanderings.

It is hard to imagine why he let the two little sisters come along that night. Years later none of them left living were able to recall the faulty logic he must have had to let them tag along. Maybe he thought if he got caught with the little sisters the punishment would be more diluted, or that he could blame them in some way. They were thrilled nonetheless and promised to be quiet and not to cry.

They waited for nightfall, then at their brother's signal they left the house, crouching and running along the cement embankment in front of their house and down onto the road. They walked for what seemed like a long time to the little sisters. They no longer recognized the houses on the road. Finally, the middle brother stopped and told them to hide in the shade of a nearby tree and to wait for him. He hissed at them to not make a sound or else, making his usual fist and shaking it at them.

After crawling under a fence and disappearing up the driveway, the middle brother found the duckling's pen, opened the cage door and scooped up an armload of ducklings. After what seemed like forever the girls saw their brother's body appear in the darkness. Then he whispered to them to run. He made it to out of the yard and onto the road. They ran for a while and then out of breath they slowed to a walk, stepping only in the middle of the road, the yellow line a place of safety from the dark edges on either side of the narrow asphalt, all of them tired and happily whispering, the baby ducklings held hidden in the fabric of the middle brother's shirt.

As they got closer to their house, the indistinct fear of their father catching them began to rise up like a thin vapor, ballooning into a hovering shape in the night sky as they reached their gravel driveway, each step a small crunch of alarm and their last hurdle to making it back into bed without Buckaflap waking up. The middle brother shushed them, a long, bent finger to his lips, the nail bed large and square like a stamp, an even line of blackened grease ever present under his nails.

They crawled into their beds, the girls falling fast

asleep in their clothes immediately while the middle boy secured the ducklings in the barn, their makeshift garage, the large space holding all the unwanted items, indecision still tugging at their father, the unfinished sorting of his old life, their old life, before their mother died, her wedding dress stuffed into an old suitcase with a faux alligator pattern, the paper edge of it beginning to peel at the corners, later damaged in the fire.

In the morning there was no explosion from Buckaflap, though they waited for it, no rant of how hard he worked and how ungrateful they were, frequently adding the threat of his substantial belt to make his point. There was just silence as he sat in his chair reading the paper. The ducklings were hidden in the barn making small chirping sounds in their make shift pen. It wasn't until later that morning when the phone rang (another rarity), the owner of the ducklings on the line, that the familiar rant from their father began.

COYOTE

The middle brother liked to play tricks and he liked risk, even though the information he amassed in almost every waking moment of his short young life told him he might want to do otherwise. Consequences didn't seem to have the right enzyme to cross into his brain. He came into the world with a strange skill set, better suited to another era. He was a wild one, a rule breaker, a natural at hotwiring cars and motorcycles and breaking into houses.

He was an excellent car mechanic, able to make most engines work, his first car a light blue Valiant with a push button transmission he bought for a hundred dollars, or maybe it was 'given' to him, eventually no one could remember the real story of the transaction. The blue Valiant was his pride and joy, its gleaming potential visible only to him in the dented fenders he covered in Bondo. His careful layering representing his high hopes and a perfect shape only he could see.

He was a natural thief and a trickster, a coyote boy who would only come in from the cold when no one was around, restless under the roof of his family home, the night air and other shady places his true home. Maybe he always knew he manifested the pain and brokenness of their family. His wild life symbolizing the wreckage they all felt, as though it was his job to carry it, to carry the rest of them through his illegal actions, the chaos he made a container created for the rest of them to be free, as though that were ever possible for any of them.

He liked to figure out how to get around any obstacle, usually just because it was there. He was drawn to the door that was closed, the challenge and the contents behind it his if he could get to them. What 'it' was, was almost beside the point. He didn't harm things out of anger usually, except for the teacher and the dog and the laxatives. It was more because he saw a way in and couldn't resist trying, a sort of *because I can* kind of attitude, the rush of the action the goal, the consequences afterwards never sticking to his skin.

He tormented his two little sisters, especially the older one. She was reliable to take the bait from him every time, crying out in surprise like it was the first infraction from him, never getting wise to him like the younger one did. He liked to hide the older sister's small plastic glasses, watching her search frantically, until in utter frustration she finally decided to tell their dad, an offense in and of itself. The glasses miraculously turned up in the silverware drawer a few minutes later, lying next to the butter knives, where she had looked several times before. She grabbed the glasses and put them on, yelling his name in an accusing wail.

They were given a toy mold maker, *Creepy Crawlers,* one Christmas that made plastic bugs when you heated up a chemical goop. The middle brother took command of it and made dozens of floppy multicolored spiders and other bugs. He occasionally hid one of the spiders in the square of mashed potatoes in the older sister's TV dinner. Their father hissing a, 'Cut it out both of you,' when it was discovered, dangling on the sister's fork. Their father glared at them, still chewing, his mouth full of Salisbury steak from the entrée triangle of his TV dinner. In that moment they both knew to stay silent, the middle brother's shoulders moving up and down with the silent laughter of winning.

When he was in eighth grade the middle brother had a disagreement with a teacher, which was a pretty regular thing at that point. It might have involved a call to their father, or a threat of expulsion, which did happen later, but whatever the reason, the middle brother was mad at this teacher and wanted revenge. The teacher always brought his dog to work. He left it in the car with the window open just enough for the dog to have circulating air but closed just enough so no pesky children's greasy fingers could get their hands in and harm the dog. He parked underneath a tree, in a shady parking spot the other teachers begrudgingly left open for him because of the dog. This was years before animal rights awareness and nobody really thought anything of the dog waiting in the car, except that maybe the teacher was a little obsessive about his dog and probably lonely.

The middle brother obtained a box of laxatives. He fed the offending teacher's dog a few of the chocolate flavored laxatives, cutting class to wait for his arrival. It is unclear whether he got caught or not, but the prank was immediately a shining legend among the four other siblings, only talked about out of earshot of their father.

CAMPING

The middle brother had pretty severe asthma as a boy—apparently all the brothers did but his was the worst—requiring frequent trips to the emergency room for bubbling treatments of medicated air. In a rare mention of their mother, their father told them that the air in Daly City had been too damp by the ocean and was one of the reasons why they, their dead mother and their father, their father conceivably a different person back then, kind and able to speak and confer with someone in a thoughtful manner, decided to move to the suburbs, into the dry hills and hot summers away from the moist grip of the ocean.

If they took a trip to a lake or a stream on one of their father's many educational nature outings, the middle brother was always late coming out to the car, hoping to be left behind as their father always threatened to do if anyone was late. But their father never left him behind for these excursions. If they were told not to go in the water or get wet, he fell in or in some way came back to their Volkswagen van soaking wet and muddy, his shoes ruined or a jacket missing or torn, surprised as anyone at the turn of events.

Their father loved camping, and later got into back-packing, a much-hated activity by all five of them. How could carrying a giant heavy pack walking up hill into mountains with no bathrooms remotely be considered fun? He joined the Mt. Diablo Hiking Club and took them on weekend camping trips up Mount Diablo, a twenty-minute drive from their house, the only peak in the area, a strange looking mountain dividing the central valley and the bay area.

These weekend trips were practice runs for the later trips to the sierras, to the high country with thinner air and speckled granite mountains. Several times on these forays into the sierras the middle brother had a night when he could not breathe, the thin air collapsing his lungs, which were still prone to asthmatic episodes in the right conditions, oxygen sliding into all the wrong places, leaving him gasping enough to have to wake their dad in the middle of the night.

The nearest hospital was usually at least an hour away. Their father, seeing the middle brother's actual distress, woke the oldest brother and told him he was going to drive the middle brother to a lower elevation where he might be able to breathe easier. He assured the oldest that he would be back as soon as he could, and he was in charge now. The rest of them were awake and listening to their father whisper, something they had never heard him do before.

Their father and the middle brother usually returned in the early morning, the four of them still in their sleeping bags curved like larvae on the slippery tent floor. The sun had yet to rise high enough to make the tent a hot square of stale air. It was still cold inside, the walls of the tent moist with condensation. They all hoped that their father would say they were going home, canceling the trip as he sometimes did since the middle brother couldn't breathe. They lay silent in the tent as they heard the loud zipper of the tent door slide up.

Sometimes when he woke them he did so almost sweetly, a gentle nudge of the arm, saying "It's time to get up," but this particular morning he was all business and they knew as a body not to argue, all arms inside for the ride. They crawled out of their sleeping bags and came out of the tent one by one, clothed in strange mixtures of space pajamas and winter coats, hair bent and pointed, standing around the wet wooden picnic table. Their father started to make breakfast, lighting the green Coleman stove, barking at the youngest brother to get the Cream of Wheat and his coffee from their supplies in the back of the car, which was always some incarnation of a VW bus, their father's chosen vehicle large enough to fit them all.

They were always hungry and ever hopeful for food other than what was on offer, especially camping food. Their dinner the night before had been a rubbery freeze-dried stroganoff and hard green apples for dessert. They wanted bacon and eggs—multiple strips of bacon, maybe four or five pieces each, and mounds of scrambled eggs—fully cooked, thick toast and soft butter amply slathered over with sweet jelly, not bitter marmalade or the clotty *Empress Strawberry Preserves* that came in a large can with a sticky lid like a paint can you had to pry open with a knife. The rest of the campsite was waking up and they could smell the delicious breakfasts that they were sure families with mothers might eat, a secret understanding and access to a world they knew nothing about, their food lust fueled by the simple greed of not having.

NUMBER FIVE

She was born a bald, robust baby with the gray eyes of a newborn that would soon change to bright blue. When her hair finally came in, it was soft and fine like dandelion fluff. She had a square forehead and no discernable eyebrows. There was a certain hint in the width between the eyes and the bridge of her nose foretelling of her indelible genetic connection to all of them. She was a tiny six-week-old infant with fresh new skin, lying quietly in a basket next to the bed the day their mother died.

It was decided that the youngest girl would go to live with their grandmother for a while after their mother died. This choice, like so many things from their childhood, is a little hazy as to what happened and why. Their grandmother was the obvious choice as she had been a foster mother to hundreds of children during the First World War, as she frequently reminded them. She had a plaque honoring her service to all those children in need on the wall of her bedroom. It was the only thing on the wall in her cloister-like bedroom. Their grandmother was English and had been a governess in China. She believed in schedules and that spoiling a child was a modern menace that must be avoided at all costs.

Their grandmother often dressed them in matching outfits and took them downtown on the 38 Geary bus which stopped right in front of the Emporium department store. Occasionally they got their picture taken by a professional photographer with a small semi-private studio deep in the interior of the Emporium. Sometimes their grandmother bought new stockings at the Emporium that came in a slim, flat, fancy looking box. She kept the delicate stockings up with industrial type garters that looked like thick rubber bands covered over with thread. Depending on where she was going, she would roll the garters just above the knee, but mostly she kept them rolled just below her knees like knee socks. Afterwards they went to Woolworths and had lunch at the counter. When she had extra money their grandmother sometimes bought them each a new hard plastic doll in a flimsy cardboard box, occasionally throwing in an outfit or a miniature baby bottle that emptied when you tilted it up, simulating feeding a real baby.

There are a few of the professional photos remaining, the two girls smiling in their various identical dresses, their little bodies slumped into each other, bangs cut high on their foreheads to last longer, their hair clean and brushed vigorously by their grandmother's claw like hand into a shiny foam curler–shaped wave.

The youngest girl came back to live with the rest of them when it was time for her to start school. No one was exactly clear why she stayed with their grandmother for so long. Memory was a particular and fickle beast, pretending to be the trusted holder of their younger moments, promising to give it all back when they needed to know.

The older sister stayed with their grandmother for long periods of time as well. But the youngest girl was quiet, her compliance probably an early choice to hide in plain sight. The older girl was a yowly creature. She often yelled and sassed back to their grandmother. Offering to care for an infant was much easier than dealing with the wild grief shooting out of the older children like sparks of electricity. Their grandmother was more accustomed to the basic needs of babies, too young to manifest their given worlds beyond hunger or having a wet diaper. Taking responsibility for the youngest the obvious choice when so much need was left unattended in the others, spilling into the stark dailiness of their lives without her.

They were referred to as *the girls*. *The girls* got a new bunk bed set when the youngest one came to stay when it was time for kindergarten. They later inherited a record player and a stack of 45s from one of the older brothers. They spent long Saturday afternoons listening to *Never On a Sunday*, pretending to be in boarding school, or on a ship far out at sea, throwing things around the room in imaginary storms. Falling into fits of laughter as they tossed around bigger and bigger things, knocking books off their bookshelves and throwing stuffed animals high into the air in the imaginary gales of wind.

Once the younger sister swallowed an ice cube while they were laughing about something. She became serious immediately, the older girl still laughing until she saw her sister lying down on her twin bed. She had stretched her body out in a straight line, her hands at her sides. She ordered the older one to cover her with a blanket. She needed to be warm if there was any hope of melting the ice cube before it harmed her. She yelled at the older sister that it wasn't funny, she could die, when her sister pantomimed exaggeratedly tucking her in with a pilly blanket and humming like one of the three stooges. The youngest somehow equated swallowing an ice cube with any number of life-threatening childhood myths, like if you swallowed a hair it would wind around your intestines and kill you, or if you swallowed a watermelon seed it would grow a melon in your stomach and kill you with its inevitable size. Swallowing rubber bands was also very dangerous, depending on their size.

The youngest girl was quiet like the youngest brother. She watched and waited, learning quickly to navigate their churning sibling mass with silence and subtle circumvention. She was smarter than all of them, out witting them all, except maybe the oldest brother. She had no trouble in school and did not get upset about much or wail dramatically when she didn't get her way. She learned early on to hold her world inside, pragmatic and ever realistic in her piloting of their family. She knew they had no mother and they had no money, the social workers that 'visited' and the afternoons spent waiting for their father's paycheck to come in the mail not lost on her.

She also knew in her wordless quiet that her birth probably killed their mother. The others never said this to her, never blamed her once, but she knew it. Maybe it was like knowing you had a lurking genetic disorder, a timetable ticking for an event, blameless and cataclysmic, even as the sun still moves across the sky, because of it nothing would ever be right.

The youngest girl loved horses, *really* loved them, in

the way that some young girls do. She had a subscription to *American Quarter Horse* from their grandmother, who seemed to think that having a magazine subscription was an essential part of being a proper child. She had a collection of realistic plastic horses that she placed on the windowsill of their bedroom window, once or twice even managing to steal a new one for her collection without getting caught. This success was quite impressive to the rest of them.

She once found an ad in the local paper for a horse for maybe a hundred or a hundred and fifty dollars, board in a stable in exchange for labor, cleaning the stalls and shoveling horse poop. It really was an incredible deal and she thought their father just might go for it. She talked about it excitedly for days, finally getting up the nerve to ask him.

She walked down the hallway from their bedroom to the living room where their father sat watching TV. The older sister waited in their bedroom, listening from the doorway. There was some murmuring and the sound of the TV and then the youngest girl's muffled voice. A loud car commercial blocked the soft answer coming from their father's mouth but the older girl could picture it, having seen the pinched smile and fake kindly tone of his *no* many times.

The younger sister came back into their bedroom, her body a block of swirling rage and disappointment. She threw herself onto her bunk. She yelled at her older sister to shut up when she asked her what happened and did something she never did: she cried herself to sleep.

BUCKAFLAP

Their father must have been weary of children: their constant complaints, their spills, their clumsy unskilled ways. He worked in Berkeley at a place he called the Rad Lab. It was affiliated with the university and was on the campus. He left for work early in the morning and when he got home in the late afternoon there they were, five little beings, their small pointed bird mouths open wide, their shiny beaks calling out to him, all chirping their empty bellied demands at him.

They could not comprehend that he might not be in the mood to figure out what to feed five kids and to have to govern the many dramas that occurred each day while he was away. He was their anchor, especially when they were small. Their need was a constant frequency that bore into him. They did not know how to see him as a person with needs of his own. He was a parent, their grown up, and they needed everything from him. It was a good night if he didn't have to take one of them to the emergency room or pick one of them up from the police station, or go to yet another parent teacher conference about one of them at their school.

He was an electronic technician for the cyclotron on campus, something to do with soldering parts together and making circuit breakers. They knew to pretend that they knew the word circuit breaker but none of them could really figure out what he did and they weren't really interested, work being a grown up thing that most grown ups complained about. There was some correlation between it and food and freedom.

Inside their father was a latent kernel of grief, an inflamed ligament of self-pity and imagined injustice coming on like the occasional flare of a bad tooth or an erupting invisible sliver burrowed deep in his skin that dug and festered its way into an unreachable ray of resentment.

He had stacks of *Scientific American* magazines on the bamboo coffee table next to his big green chair. Even in their deepest boredom most of the siblings could not find anything worth looking at in those magazines. Even the bright graphically enhanced pictures of huge atoms and colorized replicas of cold viruses that looked like science fiction planets were dead on the page as soon as they read what they really were. They felt tricked by the colors and bright detailing of the pictures, which falsely promised some make-believe action or enjoyment they could understand.

He worked with scientists and other really smart people and he wanted to be one of them, felt he was in fact one of them, if he had only been able to go to college. Their father had fought in the Second World War and could have gone to college when he got home on the GI bill. He was an only child so it is blurry as to why this didn't happen.

There were no aunts or uncles or even any friends left to hold up a mirror for them. More and more people disappeared from his life as they grew up. Some died, but most drifted away from his angry energy.

Maybe he got married to their mother right when he came home, there is no one left to ask and any questions— they did ask about the war and he shut them down immediately, the same sudden violent twist as with most questions about their mother. The two topics—the war and their mother—were taboo, understood in their collective child body as danger zones, contaminated areas that were off limits, a sure-fire way to wake the beast of his anger and get the belt for extraneous reasons.

Their father went to work for the phone company after he got back from the war and he and their mother started trying to have a family. The story goes that their father and mother had no luck getting pregnant for five long years, even going to doctors to figure it out and then wham, the babies started rolling out in to their lives and onto every available surface.

At some point he got a better job at the university, and they moved to the suburbs. They set up house in Indian Valley, a newish subdivision in Walnut Creek with five small children all a year or two apart. This was well before disposal diapers and mounds of dirty diapers routinely soaked in the toilet or hung on the line, dripping onto the flattened bare dirt of the backyard.

When their mother died one afternoon, six weeks after her last baby was born, she had complained of not feeling well. She was resting in their bedroom after lunch when a blood clot nestled somewhere in her body got loose and flew like a tiny rocket through her pumping vessels into her lungs, where it landed like a giant space ship on top of a small bird, smashing all its delicate bones, death fast and thorough moving through her body, the impact so absolute there was little intervening space in her mind to register any consciousness of leaving, no capacity of time or space to comprehend this quick ending. Did she have time to think of the five of them as she left her body, catapulted into the sky? When their father came back into their bedroom to check on her it was painstakingly clear, she was gone.

The immediate days after she died are lost to time, the devastation unreachable but deeply understood. Their grandmother came out to help with the children and soon afterwards, when the funeral and the helpful women of the neighborhood receded, there are a few scant memories of a stepmother, her tenure brief.

Her name was Charlene and they remembered her as strict and unkind, even with her own brood of four children. It was obvious what was trying to be accomplished by the marriage. Then there was another move, along with the quick disappearance of said stepmother and her passel of children.

The youngest girl went to live with their grandmother. The rest of the children stayed together with their father and the housekeepers began to arrive. Some would stay for a long time, maybe even a year or two. Some arrived, unpacked their things, made dinner and quit the same day. The first meal with a new housekeeper was always a pivotal battle ground of carefully designed bad behavior and a chaos they all joined in, enjoying each sibling's tiny victory towards their common goal of seeing if they could unravel the new housekeeper. If she made it past the first dinner she often stuck around. It was hard to know what triggered them to leave after they settled in. It might have been the violence of their fighting with each other, throwing rocks and dinner knives at each other, or it might have been the middle brother's tendency to steal from their wallets. Or it might be that they mocked and harassed a certain housekeeper's child. Things went missing, dead bugs and tiny animals appeared in the cabinets.

When the last straw happened and the last housekeeper gave up, their father had to reload the Volkswagen with her few belongings and drive the spooked housekeeper back to the Greyhound bus station.

POCKET MONEY

The older sister was frequently at the Stanton house playing with Laura Stanton when it was dinnertime. She was permitted to stay in the Laura's room while they ate. They never asked her if she wanted to have dinner with them, or maybe she was invited but told them she had already had dinner, her Pity Radar well installed.

While the Stantons ate their dinner, the older sister sat on the end of Laura Stanton's neat twin bed, her legs dangling over the end. Swinging her legs back and forth she looked around the bedroom that felt dulled in Laura's absence. It was still light outside and time seemed to stand still as the family ate in the other room. It was pretty quiet in the dining room except for the sound of a fork or knife occasionally scraping on a plate. The only voice she could make out was Mr. Stanton's and then Laura's mother's murmuring something back.

Unlike the Stantons' subdued dinner table, dinner at their house was fast and loud, the TV dinners they frequently ate placed on top of the shiny boxes they came in, the waxy cardboard flattened to serve as placemats, smeary plastic glasses of Kool-Aid positioned next to each box. When their father did cook dinner, everyone ate quickly in an attempt to get seconds, the girls never seemed to be able to compete with the wolfing older brothers. They tried, though, even when it was attempting to get the last of their father's meatloaf, which they all hated, a greyish brick of over-cooked ground beef mixed with disgusting tiny green capers, period. The older girl hated the tang of the capers, deftly moving them around in her mouth and out onto a napkin, saving and chewing the meat in her mouth.

The older sister quietly stood up and began to wander around Laura's room, touching the things on her dresser, looking in the tiny drawers of her jewelry box. Getting bolder she began opening the dresser drawers, looking at the rows of socks and neatly folded t-shirts, so different from her own drawers where she hurriedly threw in her clean clothes when she had them. In one of the drawers she discovered a pile of quarters and a few dollar bills in a small pink quilted box.

Reflex made her look around the empty room and at the bedroom door which was partially open. She was a natural thief in a family of thieves and didn't want to get caught. She tiptoed to the door, silently opened it just a crack further and looked out into the hallway where she heard the father's voice droning on in the dining room. Then she came back into Laura's room and took a few quarters from the drawer and put them quickly into the pocket of her shorts, leaving the dollars in the box. She jumped back onto the bed and resumed swinging her legs until Laura was finished with dinner. Heading home at dusk she squeezed her fingers around the coins as she skipped up her driveway. They became more hers as she got closer to her house.

One night that summer Mr. Stanton decided to peek in on the older sister while she was waiting for Laura. He saw her taking something out of his daughter's dresser drawer and putting it into her pocket. Maybe Laura had complained about her money going missing, maybe he had a hunch. She had tried to mix it up, not stealing money every time she waited for Laura but the pull was too strong, her ability to get her hands on any money was pretty much non-existent.

Mr. Stanton did not confront her in the act but came up to her after the family had finished dinner and they were all watching *Animal Kingdom* in the den. The two girls sat side by side on the plaid couch. Mr. Stanton's head appeared in the doorway looking right at her. She felt a rising panic when his head asked to speak with her. It was extremely rare that grown ups talked directly to children, and fathers even less so than mothers.

His tone was veiled and smarmy as he talked to her in the hallway. He wanted to know if she knew what stealing was, did she know it was wrong and not what good people do? He finished with the suggestion that it might be best if she didn't come over for a while, okay good night then. She left the house without saying good bye to Laura. She walked down the driveway and into the street quickly like a low-bellied cat, running across the road, looking at the neighboring houses as she fled for home. Did they all know what she did, would Mr. Stanton call her father and tell him? Mulling over this probability she opened the screened back door and slid into her room to wait it out. She decided that if Laura's father didn't call in the next day or two, she was probably safe.

STANLEY HOUSE

Life in the days following the barn fire is another dead zone of memory, the details mostly forgotten. The crucial conversations that must have taken place that first night are unknowable. Did they all sleep in the farmhouse that night, the smell of wet burned wood and smoke in the fabric of the curtains, lingering in the furniture, in the bedclothes? Their father decided that the girls (always referred to as a single unit) would go to go stay with their grandmother in San Francisco for a while. She lived in a cold spotless apartment on Spruce Street in the inner Richmond district, living a cloistered existence of early mornings for no reason and a strict bedtime in what seemed like broad daylight.

The sisters used to like going to stay with their grandmother when they were little. It was quiet and clean at their grandmother's apartment. There was a certain sense of routine and safety they could not possibly have articulated their need for. They felt comfort in the smell of the clean sheets dried on the clothes line out her backdoor and in the Yardley's lavender soap their grandma kept in her drawers to make her clothes smell good.

At their grandmother's they were safe from the relentless pecking order and fighting with their brothers. There was no winning with them and they as the youngest were always going to be the bottom of the heap. At their grandmother's house there was better food and more of it, even though their grandmother was English and she boiled her meat into tastelessness instead of cooking it, food was still coming forth regularly, hot food and someone else was preparing it and cleaning up the dishes afterwards.

Their grandmother liked to make bread pudding for dessert, pretending she was making it for them as her Puritan ways allowed for no moments of pleasure or want. She made her bread pudding with the soft airy raisin bread from the super market like it was an exotic treat. The stacked bread slices, even after sitting in the oven for what seemed like hours came out soggy and damp, the delicious smell of cinnamon a betrayal, the milky bread often tepid in the middle. As they watched her make it in the afternoon the older girl tried to will their grandma with her mind not to pour in so much milk, begging her silently in her head to stop before the bread disappeared into the pool of milk. She was shocked to see what real bread pudding looked like years later in a café, solid and dry like a piece of tall cake.

Their grandmother washed her clothes in the bathtub even after she moved to an apartment on the level part of Spruce Street that had a washer and drier in the basement. She had survived both wars, and she couldn't help it. She tried a few times to approach the washing machine in the basement. She touched the cold white lid, looking inside the machine, then over at the dials and couldn't comprehend the language of its choices. What was permanent press, what was delicate? She put the lid down carefully with the edge of her palm and walked away, making a sweeping dismissive gesture with her hand as she went for the stairs, basket of dirty clothes in hand.

They lost the house after the barn fire, their father let it go into foreclosure, and they moved into a two-bedroom apartment along a busy industrial road in another sub-urban town. The barn fire was the last straw for their father who, as it turned out, was behind on the mortgage in a significant way. In some kind of financial arithmetic the fire was the sum of the equation, the other side of the equal sign to let everything drop away, falling into the charred weeds near the collapsed barn, the unopened bank statements that had continued to gather, landing like thin white leaves, the red writing in the small cellophane window disappearing, settling like a stone into a creek bed, falling forgotten into a silent silty pile on the table next to their father's green chair.

The middle brother never made it to high school and was sent away to Hanna Boys Center after the fire, a thinly veiled name for reform school, a home for *troubled boys* it said on the beige brochure with a drawing of a group of boys looking sappy and compliant on the front cover. The middle brother never lived at the Stanley House apart-ments. There was no space there for him, no bedroom, no bed, only the couch in the living room, which frequently held a pile of laundry waiting to be folded, taking up half of the couch. The pile often functioned as an armrest or pillow for one of them when they watched TV. When the clothes in the pile finally got folded, they looked crumpled and useless.

The oldest brother, who was already in high school and had grown tall and lean and handsomely blond, had to share a room with their father in the cramped two-bedroom apartment. He put up a nubby beige bedspread in an attempt to separate the space from his father who was growing larger every year, his body firm and round in the middle like whichever one was the fat one from Laurel and Hardy. The youngest brother and the girls shared the other bedroom, a set of bunk beds and a small twin bed filling the tiny bedroom. They would often fight, massively, violently, pulling the mattresses off each other's beds, throwing the wad of bedclothes into a heap, screaming insults and sweating into exhaustion onto the mixed-up heap on the floor.

They would never know for sure whether the middle brother started the fire that day. He might have been playing with firecrackers with the Stanton boy, launching M-8os or some other illegal and thus valuable kind of contraband, the obtaining of it alone giving him a strange self-worth. Regardless of the truth of who did it, there was a seismic shift and reformation of their family after the fire.

Their father routinely threatened all of them, especially the two older boys, that he should just send them all to foster care. This threat was usually pulled out when he had to get one of them out of juvenile hall or the police had called wanting to question them about a robbery of a store or the theft of a car. Admittedly the middle brother had learned how to hot wire a car in middle school and couldn't help himself sometimes. He would occasionally hotwire the oldest brother's motor-cycle if he saw it parked somewhere in town if he had somewhere to be, leaving the oldest stranded and fuming.

With the threat of being sent to foster care long ago lodged in their minds, all of them wondered if this was that moment. They wondered out loud if they were going home at all. They practiced scenarios, looking for holes in their ideas or worse, plausibility. The girls were relieved for once to be put on the Greyhound Bus to their grand-mother's house, whispering in bed to each other in their grandmother's tiny bedroom, a camping cot set up next to her twin bed. The girls took turns sleeping in the hard twin bed or on the cot, a canvas and metal thing with the cold bars of the sides ever present and numbing their legs and arms when they fell asleep. When they stayed with their grandmother, she slept on the couch, insisting on calling it the Chesterfield, which they guessed was English for couch.

They sometimes wished they could just be sent to boarding school, like out of the Shirley Temple movies they loved to watch. Their grandmother mentioned boar-ding school a lot when they were younger, as some kind of proper place where rich people sent their children to be educated the right way, with lots of discipline and shame. She loved the Irish Store at the bottom of Spruce Street. She often paused to peer in the dusty windows before starting up the steep hill to her apartment. The Irish Store never appeared to be open, the window display consisting of a faded set of cardboard of Irish dancers and a tarnished silver tea set. To the side of the cardboard dancers was a placard for the Irish Sweepstakes, listing dates and winnings in tiny black print. Their extremely practical and frugal grandmother bought a sweepstakes ticket there regularly, promising to send them to boarding school if she won, dreamily describing what she would do with her winnings with a shiny eyed look that might have been desire, but they rarely saw such a thing in her face and could not be sure.

LATCH KEYS

They were latch-key kids long before the term was used. They got themselves up and dressed in the morning, sometimes picking up and putting on dirty wrinkled clothes off the floor of their rooms and heading to the kitchen, ever hopeful something good to eat might have manifested in the middle of the night. They usually made themselves an Instant Breakfast with powered milk or ate cereal if there was any. Often, they went directly to school, not hungry enough to bother. By midmorning they were always surprised when their bellies throbbed with a hunger that made them nauseous.

They were on the school lunch program, so they knew they would eat lunch. They stood in line with the other kids, laughing and sliding the metal trays along the rail, their free lunch secret safe from the other kids. They walked home on their own, roaming the neighborhood, fighting with each other until their father came home. They had learned to wait wordlessly as he came into the house, watching for any clue as to what kind of dinner would manifest from their father, always exhausted and at best silent when he came home, falling into his big vinyl green chair which made sliding sounds and exhaled loudly with his body's landing.

Before the fire, they attended Walnut Heights Elementary, the small neighborhood school a few blocks down the road from their house. The school was a pivotal landmark in their childhood lives. They spent many hours in school and after school was over, its familiar grounds were an extension of their world. They played on the jungle gym and the swings after school and on the weekends. They rode their bikes at the school where they shouldn't, the middle brother riding his bike down a small set of stairs repeatedly, trying to pop a wheelie while doing so without much success. They roamed the empty outside halls and climbed on the roof. In the spring there were softball games in the evening at the baseball diamond. A man appeared every season with an ice cooler selling cans of Craigmont sodas from Safeway, and in the summer there was summer camp, one open classroom with art supplies and free breakfast and snacks, reason enough to go.

Behind the first section of classes were two small courtyards with gray weathered wood planters filled with tiny trees that never seemed to grow any larger. These squares of asphalt were empty of playing children during recess as their only function was to punish children or to help teachers with some risky construction paper art project that required some kind of spraying or fumes. The oldest girl often spent recesses there in the small squared off plot. Her second grade teacher Mrs. Hickman, pretty and stylish, sighed as she sentenced her to another recess in the 'quad.' Mrs. Hickman later began taking the two sisters home to stay the weekend with her and her two daughters.

When the oldest girl was in third grade there was a girl in her class who was diabetic. Her name was Rebecca and she and the oldest girl became fast friends, assigned to sit next to each other at the beginning of the school year. Rebecca had a little sister the same age as the younger sister, and Rebecca's family seamlessly folded the girls into their family. Both girls often spent the weekend with Rebecca's family. They had a large paneled rec room and a record player. They listened to Herb Alpert and played a complicated game with pillows and crazy dancing and trying to not touch the floor. At night before bed they had *gute*, a small snack, which Rebecca's dad told them meant *to eat* in some foreign language. The purpose of this was to help Rebecca avoid low blood sugar in the middle of the night. The father made it a game, singing silly songs and sometimes talking in funny voices. None of them cared that much about Rebecca's blood sugar, they didn't understand her being a diabetic, they only knew that sometimes she got moody and faded away until she got something sweet to eat or drink. They just liked getting a treat before bed.

Rebecca's parents had made an agreement with Rebecca's teacher, and in a drawer at the back of the classroom was a box of sugar cubes for her for to have when she felt that 'funny' feeling of impending low blood sugar. One afternoon after school the oldest girl was walking along the back wall of classrooms on her way home. She habitually checked the classroom doors as she roamed, something she saw her brothers do. This time she got lucky and noticed that the door to her classroom was unlocked.

She was stalling going home that afternoon, knowing she hadn't done the laundry like her father asked her to do. She knew she wasn't going to rush home and do it. That time had passed, vaporizing into its own inertia, the imaginary time of action now frozen someplace away from her body. The wrath of her father was a routine predicted storm system, and you just got through it. Like weather, there was also the remote possibility the meteorologists got it wrong, weather being weather and by definition able to change its mind or magically disappear without notice. He might not notice, collapsing into his chair to watch the news. She snuck into the classroom and made a beeline for the drawer at the back of the classroom and ate all Rebecca's sugar cubes in the pink and white C&H box. Her father remembered about the laundry and made her skip watching TV to do it.

LETTERS

Their father and mother were the only children of immigrant parents. How both sets of parents ended up in California is now long forgotten. Their father's parents were from England. They met when they both were working in China after the First World War. Their grandmother, later of the practical white polished shoes cracked from her bunions, was employed there as a governess for a wealthy English family. She was twenty-nine when she married their grandfather and her passport gave her occupation as *spinster*.

Their grandfather was an accountant and worked with an English railroad company in China. They returned to England to get married. In one of the few photos of that day they are both wearing traditional Chinese clothing, even though when they lived in China they only associated with other expats and their grandmother prided herself on never having eaten Chinese food.

Their mother's parents were from Ireland. Both of their mother's parents were dead before any of their grandchildren were born. There was no curious family genealogist among them, no history buff who found it all so interesting. The five of them were of the opposite nature. They learned early to not talk about their mother or her family; questions or references to her were met with a wide silence or even anger from their father. The death of their mother became the unseen pall over their lives, with them at each meal, with them at school and playing with other kids. They were living without her, moving through every day, no words adequate to convey the grief grown into their bones.

The folklore that did exist about their parents was that they grew up together in Berkeley. The two sets of immigrant parents shared a backyard fence and their mothers became good friends, both of them probably glad to have someone to talk to who wasn't an overly cheerful American, bending and twisting the language every time they opened their mouths. Their father's mother liked to tell them that their mother and father played together as little kids, walking to the neighborhood park or running around in the backyard while their mothers gossiped and hung out the wash.

After high school their father joined the army and ended up stationed in the Pacific. When he came back he was different, as so many of the returning soldiers were. He was prone to long silences and had an increasingly bad temper, which their grandmother took to calling his 'flare ups.' He had dark, sporadic outbursts of rage and did not want to talk about the war when prodded.

Their mother was one of the few people in his post war world he did not take issue with. He enjoyed her stopping in to lend him a book or to drop off a pie her mother just baked. His face lit up with a grin and he suddenly became chatty and friendly when she came over. His mother's eyes were wide as she walked down the hall to the kitchen with the pie, to leave them alone.

He felt the obvious comfort of knowing her for so long but he was also stunned to see what a tall gorgeous brunette she had become. Her eyes were a deep dark brown and she smiled easily and laughed a lot, whether he was grouchy or not. She was free, unencumbered by the presence of the smothering anger in which he so often dwelled.

My darling,

I just wanted you to get some mail in our new home and I have been thinking how wonderful you are and how very much I love you. Since I can't tell you this minute that I love you more than anyone else in the world, you'll have to wait until Monday.

All my love always,

M.

P.S.   Gee, I love you xxx

Mrs. Crane had always been there in their lives it seemed, an amorphous person talking on the other end of the phone with their grandmother. The thick black phone hardly ever rang, so it was an event when it did. Their grandmother's apartment was often punitively quiet and spotless in case of visitors who never came, or maybe it was their grandmother's old-world austerity, born of the wars and being one of many in a poor family. Or maybe it was her need to scrub away the hidden remorse of being born a woman, murky and unworthy with her first breath in a world of men with control over every aspect of her life. Cleaning was a shield, a momentary action that could be done to set it all right. Cleaning was a way to tire her arms, her back, it was a way to lower the volume on the smallness that was her life.

Their mother knew the formless Mrs. Crane as well. Many years after their mother died, decades in fact, Charlene, very briefly their stepmother so long ago, sent a large envelop to the youngest brother, filled with letters their mother had written to Mrs. Crane. It was obvious Charlene had read them all, correcting any mistakes she saw in the letters with a faint red pencil.

When the youngest brother received the package from Charlene, he called the siblings and told them about the letters. They all gathered at the oldest brother's house on Mer-lot Street, except the middle brother. The youngest girl read the letters out loud while their various children played around them, running in and out of the patio door, chasing a bewildered tiny dog when the adults weren't watching.

There was a sense in that sunny room on that ordinary, uneventful Saturday of an intense collective listening, the listening of children, still and quiet in their seats, mesmerized by the story. That day each of them was listening for their name, listening hard for any mention of them, made whole again just for a moment by the light of her voice written into the page, speaking of them when she was still alive and they still belonged to her.

As the youngest girl read the letters, they all laughed and smiled at the funny stories their mother told Mrs. Crane of them as little babies. The youngest girl smiled too, as they called out each other's names when they were mentioned. One of brothers asked, where are the girls? The youngest said she didn't think she would be in any of the letters. They got quiet for a moment, all of them knowing the time line and that their mother died a few weeks after she was born. But there she was in the last letter, the last baby born, carefully placed on the dining room table and tied with a pink ribbon, while their mother wrote a letter to Mrs. Crane.

Dear Mrs. Crane,

I'm sorry it has been so long since I've written to you. The oldest is walking now and climbing everywhere so it is hard to take my eyes off of him. His father just got him a little wooden bench so he can climb up and help me cook and wash the dishes. He loves to move the faucet back and forth. He gets confused when I rinse the plates and try to put them in the dish rack, he cries because he thinks our game is over.

His father is trying to get on at PG&E but for now is still working nights at the phone company until he gets an interview. Hope to visit soon.

Best,

M.

Dear Mrs. Crane,

Hello, hope you are feeling better. The baby is almost due and his father has been building and painting like a mad man. I hope it is a boy so they can share the room he is toiling over! I have a pile of good boys clothes from our first who is talking nonstop and making complicated battles at sea in the bathroom sink at bath time.

Sincerely,

M.

Dear Mrs. Crane,

Our second son is here! He arrived a few weeks ago with a head of dark hair like mine. The oldest doesn't know what to make of him just yet, he thinks he is boring and sleeps too much, both things I am grateful for! It is good that their father works nights so he can help when he wakes up but keeping the children quiet in the morning is difficult, especially when it is rainy and we can't go out to the park. I look forward to hearing from you.

Best,

M.

Dear Mrs. Crane,

I just got back from the doctor and it looks like we are going to have another baby! I am thrilled and a little nervous, as two is such a handful! The oldest boy is a sweet little man and helps with the baby so much, they are inseparable. He knows what the baby wants before I do and translates his baby talk for me. My husband has an interview with UC Berkeley next week. It would be the day shift, hooray! Cross your fingers.

Best,

M.

Dear Mrs. Crane,

Thank you for the rocking horse. The second boy can barely reach the footholds but he can still get it going pretty fast. He ducks his head down like a racecar driver, holding on and laughing. The youngest boy watches him, holding onto the couch wiggling back and forth along with him. I had to take our second boy to Dr. White twice last month for his asthma. I will be glad for the warmer weather to dry things up so he can breathe at night and we can sleep!

Yours,

M.

Dear Mrs. Crane,

It's been a while I am sad to say, I hope you can forgive me. I appreciate your letters so much, they make my life as a mother so much brighter. My husband got the job at the cyclotron at UC Berkeley so he is commuting into Berkeley every day. Luckily, he leaves early before the traffic and gets off at three before the other commuters get started at four or five. He is driving the old Volkswagen bus, so I hope it holds up!

We went camping a few weeks ago and slept in our tent in the redwoods. We took the playpen and the boys did fine, B and K came out for the day and we had a fine picnic while the boys slept.

I hope this letter finds you well,

Fondly,

M.

Dear Mrs. Crane,

We have been in the thick of it over here. The baby was crawling in the living room and my husband must have not seen him and tripped over him and fell and broke his ankle. Then a week later the baby bit his father's big toe, which was a juicy looking toy sticking out of his cast. There was a lot of ruckus and the poor little baby didn't know what he did wrong!

I am surrounded by all my men who are terribly cranky at the moment. My husband will get the cast off in a few weeks so he is off work and at home, not really able to help out much with his foot in a cast. I relish naptime and adhere to it strictly!

Best,

M.

Dear Mrs. Crane,

We had a scare with our second son who had to stay in the hospital for two nights with pneumonia! The damp weather here is not kind to my boys I'm afraid. He is home now and doing much better, running and wrestling with the oldest who is sweet with him and sometimes lets him win a round or two.

Fondly,

M.

Dear Mrs. Crane,

It was so nice to see you last week! The boys just love you. What a pleasure to have you visit our little pre-school! I hope the trip wasn't too tiring. I'm feeling pretty well this time, the pregnancy is flying by, as I'm so busy with the boys. Maybe this one will be a girl.

Thank you as always for your wise words, I don't think you know how much you help me. See you at the next Christening!

Fondly,

M.

Dear Mrs. Crane,

Well our first daughter has broken the spell of baby boys! She has greenish eyes and absolutely no hair! I think she looks like the oldest boy. I'm not sure what to do with a girl baby, but we will try! Thank you for your lovely card and flowers, it was so kind of you to think of me after all these babies.

Best,

M.

Dear Mrs. Crane,

Thank you for coming to our daughter's Christening. The day was so nice and I have to admit that I love dressing a girl. The booties you gave her are so dear, wait until you see her wearing them in the professional photos, fancy! The boys ate too much cake, and Robert's mother was fussing at each spill. She and their grandfather came over early and stayed late. She was a big help really. Thank you again for everything.

Fondly,

M.

Dear Mrs. Crane,

I am trying to get this letter off to you, as it has been too long. Our second daughter is allowing me to write to you, at least for the moment. She is on the dining room table right next to me, tied with a pink ribbon, in a rare moment of quiet. Her hair is sparse and looks like pure white fuzz and her eyes are her father's blue. The new neighborhood is lovely and the weather is so different, much better for the boys' asthma. School will be out in a few weeks and the wild boys will need distraction. I think it is time for swimming lessons and there is a local pool so that is hopefully the plan.

Fondly,
M.

The oldest boy held the most of her memory in his cells. His time with her as the firstborn created a different etching into his life, into his way of being. But, over the years he had only one memory left, a memory of her in a blue polka dot dress, talking to him as she put something in the closet and closed the door. He remembered only the tone of her words, her kindness an energy he held onto almost as tightly as he held on to the need to remember her face.

He remembered the day when he couldn't call up her face anymore. She had been slowly fading over the bleak days and years, even though he thought about her constantly, devotedly every day. When their father died so many years later, he finally stopped thinking about her every day. Then he felt a sense of resolution, a feeling of an old order being slipped back into place that made him secretly feel safe and whole, knowing his parents were together as if that were the key that had been missing all these years.

It was mid-afternoon, a sunny day. When he thought about that day, the oldest brother always remembered that the temperature was perfect. Their mother had just fixed them lunch. She tidied up the dishes and told their father she didn't feel well and was going to lie down. He went to check on her a while later and the oldest brother followed him, standing in the doorway, looking at his mother on the bed. Her eyes were rolled up in her head and his father was holding her limp body. His father yelled at him to get out. He told him to run across the street and get the neighbor, Mr. Bradford. He ran across the street without looking, thinking of his mother, hearing her voice telling him to always look both ways. He felt guilty for disobeying her, unsure whether he would tell her later when they talked before bed. He beat his little fists hard on the door until Mr. Bradford came to the door looking annoyed and then panicked as the oldest boy yelled at him over and over that they needed to get help, something's wrong with our mom.

CHIMERA

The brain has always been a strange place for those who study it. And memory is one of its strangest tenants. Memories in the brain seem to whir continually, folding and sifting from brain stem to hippocampus and back, ant-like in their activity, categorizing incoming reality, constantly decoding what is essential to keep, stacking the amassing fragments like sandbags on a levee, tagging and labeling the various events, shelved in a dusty indecipherable order like an evidence room in a police basement.

It is believed that the brain stores all our moments, kept in silence; the feel of the wind on that certain day of disappointment, the image of someone's hair, an arch of the eyebrows. A place is found for any and all furtive details, memory's classification system quirky in the daylight and other worldly in its moments of unexplainable synchronicity. When a face, the angle of the light, the shape of a hand, all for a moment feel oddly like reuniting with a missing part of us, a place we've been before, an infant amnesia momentarily deciphered, its meaning necessary to finish the task of being. Facts, so called, entangled in the sheets of memory, like a mother of infant twins who must paint the fingernail of one of the babies in the early days to tell the two apart until animal knowing kicks in.

Children's brains are even trickier then, their smoother surface has less cavernously lodged surface area, fewer context clues have made their way in to help translate, precious few landmarks are tucked up into the gray blind alleys that will develop later to aid the child brain in understanding the world in which they find themselves. The brain of a child is filling, swiftly and imperceptibly, like a fast tide coming in, the gray matter soaking up life in its curling shore of gray clay.

In the storied reckonings continually received, the naturally anxious consciousness yearns for closure, a period placed at the end of all those free-floating fragments. The brain is motivated by its primitive need to know what comes next. Like some vestige of days on the savannah or deep in the forest, being both prey and preyed upon. If a task is interrupted the brain will remember it and want to do anything possible to finish it, the undone task much more clearly remembered than anything completed, filed away as memory. The brain continues to push and rev even if it is begged to stop by the sleepless cries of the psyche.

This need for completion of every synaptic firing tossed out, every loose filament floundering in the landscape of the brain may be why the siblings held the memory of their mother with a kind of feral sacredness that they did not have the language to speak. They felt compelled in their sibling body, their mass of arms and legs, to hold close the idea of her, their mother a sacred deity, her memory a negative space of violent interruption, a place of no longer.

They gripped her essence tight, a hallowed necessity. They were her biggest unfinished task and she theirs, the moment of her death the point of interference, the point of impossible dissolution of each one of them, fragmented, soft shelled and in need of protection, of her hands and arms to touch them and shape them. They all needed more time with her to finish the task of them. Her death was described to them by the adults like some kind of a disappearance, almost like a lost object. But they experienced her leaving as an epic vanishing of their guide, their one true heart, their ultimate place of love and home and safety. They didn't have the words to describe these feelings of the simultaneous rupture in their little bodies. It was mysterious to them how they were still able to walk and cry and bleed like any other day, when their axis had fallen so completely.

Her death that warm afternoon felt like it was being described to them in hieroglyphic terms they did not understand. They did not know the carved-up cave symbol for dead, for grief, for the finality of death. The ensuing pain a strange terrible message from the world of adults, adults who had the power and the defusing ability of grown up words that didn't convey information so much as hide in plain sight the harder meanings no one wants to acknowledge.

The various adults tasked with telling them, bestowing on them, her five little children, the horrific shift that was now their life without her, stumbled. These well-meaning adults delivered the truth of her death from a complicated place they knew they didn't really understand or inhabit themselves, nor did they ever want to. These adults talked in vague cloud shapes, saying things like *heaven* and *gone and not coming back* and *please stop crying.*

Memory is a swelter, a chimeral ray that will tell its victim anything. It tells the eyes, who abide quite simply, what they see as they flip the image, signaling to the optic nerve, synapsing with the rest of the brain. Consciousness is the restless agent, the twitchy manager of the building, spinning all it can reach, needing ownership of all images and drama, convinced of the necessity to believe that what is remembered is absolute fact, not lore, or gut felt or fear driven, not a roiling in a sky that never was there in the first place. Memory is a faulty fact checker, the life it interprets classified as documentary, a filmic arbiter of truth, as though truth were not a rare and esoteric idea annoying and intangible, its definition shy like a wolf. In the end the truth that matters is how it feels.

HANNA BOYS CENTER

The middle brother left behind a cigar box from Emil's Villa when he died, the rib place their dad liked to go to on payday. At the end of the waiting area was a large chrome cash register sitting on top of a glass display case, filled with miniature ceramic and metal pigs, breath mints and rows of cigars in open colorfully embossed cardboard cigar boxes with gold paper edges. The shiny small bands around the brown leafy bodies of the cigars made them look partially clothed, like cartoon characters waiting in their orderly box. A large gray-haired hostess named Grace saved the boxes for them and they took turns getting a fresh empty cigar box that smelled strange and plantlike, sweet and bitter.

Inside the cigar box were old letters from his father and his grandmother written to him when he was sent to Hanna Boys Center. There were also a few photos, some carefully torn out newspaper clippings, one an ad for a slingshot and one ad for a tiny motorized bike. There was also a rosary slipping around in the bottom of the box. Included in the papers and photos was a faded pamphlet from Hanna Boys Center, the boys' home where he was

84

sent to live for several years after the barn burned down. His siblings called it what it was to them, reform school, but never in front of the middle brother as it made him start into his tirade about how unfair it all was and that he didn't burn down the barn. On the cover of the pamphlet was a simple black and white drawing of the layout of the Center, depicting a serene and orderly valley nestled in the low hills of Sonoma County. The buildings were rudimentary single-story boxes with tiny squares of windows that look like perfect square teeth. There were two-minute stick figures walking a dog down the road. In the foreground of the drawing there is a boy sitting in the shade of a tree, also with a dog. There are neatly farmed fields in the background, tall thin cypress trees and dark curling bushes near the school and the gymnasium. Dogs were not allowed at Hanna Boys Center.

The oldest brother and the older sister went through the cigar box together one afternoon. Its random arrival an oddity like the letters from their mother. The box was a new layer of their sparse past appearing like a mystical visit from their brother. The contents of the box not looked for, its existence unknown before that afternoon. The oldest brother pulled out the pamphlet for Hanna Boys Center. He wondered why the middle brother would keep the brochure of somewhere he had been banished to so long ago. It seemed oddly out of place with all the other personal items of their brother's time there. The older sister began to read the pamphlet out loud.

Dedicated. . .

With grateful appreciation to the many thousands of Westerners of good will who by their sacrifices have built and are maintaining Hanna Center as a haven for neglected boys of all races and creeds.

Hanna Center came into being in the mid-1940s, when more and more youngsters, most of them products of broken homes, were left without adult guidance and care so necessary to all children.

The effort is made to reach out for the bewildered boy who has faced problems beyond the capacity of his young mind and heart. . . and to give him the care and affection and direction, which will make his life a credit to his God and his country.

The next page of the brochure is a full-page drawing of just the head of a young blond boy. He is looking sky ward, open-faced, he appears to be searching, his mouth is slightly open, his eyes large and saccharine. His is a gaze that says he is so very grateful for the help offered from Hanna Boys Center. The boy is wearing a white shirt collar, the rest of his shirt and body disappearing into the black space of the rest of the page.

The forgotten boy—the boy who had no home or for one reason or another could not live in his home—was the inspiration for the founding of our little "town."

"The 'boys' town' of the West" Sonoma California, *(707) 996-6767*

On the next page of the brochure there are pictures of some famous men of the day taken with residents of the Center. It isn't clear whether the men themselves were once residents or if they are just benefactors posing for some routine publicity shots, displaying concrete evidence of their giving back to the community.

Ernie Ford is playing the piano and looking up kindly at a young boy in an oversized suit jacket sitting on the piano. Jimmy Durante is smiling for the camera with two boys looking on. Durante has a piece of paper in his hand and is wearing a large dark hat tilted off to one side of his head. His hand and exposed arm is thick with veins and hair and he wears a black wristwatch. One of the boys in the photo with him is brown skinned.

There is a picture of Willie Mays who is smiling at the camera in his Giants uniform while a boy in a plaid shirt holds a bat ready to swing. The boy is grinning widely at Willie Mays. Placed in the middle of the photos is a drawing of a map of California, the bay area is in focus with an emblem for Hanna Boys Center and a small circular drawing of three smiling boys of varying ages. They appear to be in casual shirts, ready for the day at Hanna Boys Center.

The pamphlet felt hot in her hand after the older sister read it. She knew she had no power to stop anything that happened to the middle brother, none of them did. But she felt guilty anyway, like she somehow betrayed him. When they were small they all had a bond, they were a formation, held together by the fear of their father and their need to guard their secret child world from grown ups, especially *their* grown up, Buckaflap. She put the brochure back into the cigar box and fished out one of the letters from them.

Dear son,

We all miss you and are looking forward to seeing you on the first Sunday of September. I have given grandmother your address so that she and the girls can write to you. Your rat is doing fine. I released the pigeons and, so far, they have not come back.

Please write and let me know what to bring when I come up—also, what kind of picnic lunch to bring. Do they have a radio club? No news on the house yet. I will have something definite by Sunday this week.

Dad and the boys send all their love,

Dad

Their father had already been seriously considering what to do about the middle brother before the barn caught on fire. The idea of sending the middle brother to Hanna Boys Center was well on its way to being formulated. He had been arrested too many times and missed so much school that social services had made the call and decided to place him 'outside the home.' The fire made the decision clearer, even though no one ever proved that he did it. The middle brother was guilty of everything by that time, and setting the fire wasn't an unreasonable assumption to make about him.

The girls were sent to their grandmother's house in San Francisco while their father tried to sort everything out. The idea of walking away from the mortgage had been slowly surfacing, at first in small disappearing flickers and then with more and longer sightings, the notion of getting rid of the house creating a spaciousness in his body. There was a current forming in his brain, a familiar default setting since losing his wife, to just drop everything, letting more and more givens just fall away. Giving the house back to the bank began to make perfect sense to him. The fire seemed an ideal collision of blamelessness, the right moment to walk away from the burden of the house and the nosy neighbors trying manage his children and him. He wanted to disappear into a new place where no one knew him, to rest just for a little while.

Dear son,

I miss you very much. I am sorry that I have not written sooner.

We have sold the house and moved to an apartment in Concord. It took about twenty trips in the car to move everything. The new address is:

1801 Monument Blvd
Apt. C-7
Concord, Calif. 94520

We have two bedrooms, a large living room, a small fenced patio. Also, there is a small swimming pool.

Your older brother will be going to Ygnacio Valley High School. The girls will be going to Fair Oaks School with Bittsey.

I will bring your radio kit, 50' of wire, and watermelon when we come up to see you the first Sunday in September.

Grandma's address is:
784 Spruce St.
San Francisco, Calif. 94118

For a few days there were three pigeons in the coop but I left the door open and did not feed them and now they have left.

There have been several big grass fires on Mt. Diablo and the hills along the freeway.

Please let me know what the rules are regarding your

making phone calls to me. I do not have a phone at the apartment but there are coin phones that you could call me on if I know the exact time you would call.

With love from everyone,

Dad

In the old cigar box were some photographs. They were square and some of them had old timey white scalloped borders around the edges. Two of the pictures are of two blurry birds, far away in the sky, nothing else. There is another picture of four birds sitting on the roof of their old house, the chimney and the TV antenna in the corner of the frame. At first glance the photos of the birds look like accidental photos, as though taken by a child, inexperienced with the workings of a camera.

The birds in the photos were the middle brother's pigeons that he raised and trained in a pigeon coop in the back yard. Someone took pictures of the pigeons and sent them to him. It most likely was the youngest sister who sent the photos, outraged at their father for just letting the pigeons go free, heartlessly cutting off their food supply and leaving them to fend for themselves.

She could only bear so much slipping away of everything in their former lives. They had lost so much already. The pigeons seemed a pointless cruelty, even as part of her knew there was no other way. Whoever bought their house would probably hate pigeons and tear down their coop anyway. Sending the middle brother pictures of his pigeons was her way of telling him he still mattered, he was still a part of their family, at least always part of their child tribe, the melded body of the five of them. He was never going to be expelled out into the dark even if he was sent away by their father and the social workers and the police.

Also in the cigar box was a picture of the next door neighbor's fence surrounded by trees. Again, at first glance there is nothing photo worthy to see in the picture. But they all had scaled that fence at least once a day, deftly balancing the toes of their tennis shoes on the tiny lip of the horizontal wood slates to hoist themselves over. They climbed over the fence to play with the Troutner kids, a family with three children who lived on the other side of the fence. Or they climbed over it to take a short cut to the streets and fields behind the Troutner's house. The fence was a thoroughfare in their child world, the picture evoking a simpler time when even trouble was easier to get through, just scale the fence and run down the street into the tall grass.

The last photo in the cigar box is of the girls. They are small, maybe eight and nine. It is summer and they are in shorts. They are standing in the backyard near the giant black cherry tree. Their father's little house where he slept at night when they were older, a mother-in-law's cottage, is in the edge of the picture. The roof is white and over exposed on the sunny day. The youngest girl is looking down, putting her hair behind her ear.

Their last summer in the house on Walnut Blvd was one of long heat filled days, the dream like torpor of time erupting into a stark close up with the barn fire and the equally sudden fallout afterwards, swift and unassailable. Buckaflap had spoken.

The middle brother was the wayward guilty son, his body the body, the life that had to be sacrificed, manifesting the collapse of their family after their mother's death. He was the catalyst, the holder of their saga, the scribe merely transmitting the shape of pain that held them all together, symbiotic, like slow killing moss on a tree, or scaly hitchhiking creatures spreading out further and further on the body of a large blind fish, unable to see or change anything. Maybe their mother was sorry for making him the carrier of all that befell their family. Maybe he knew it was what he had to do from the very moment of his birth, that it all was set in motion, descent of dust and men and ships and war, and crying mothers losing so many children.

Dear brother,

I am sorry to see you go. We are staying at Grandma's. Maybe we'll visit you sometime. Scholl will open soon, hope you have many friends.

Love your sister,

P.

age 10 1/2

Dear brother,

We go home on Wed. to the apartment. We've gone babysitting a lot with Grandma. How are you? I'm fine. What have you been doing lately.

Love

M. Your sister

age 9 1/2

P.S. (Write Back Please!)

The letters from the girls were the hardest to read, their letters always arriving together. They were still so young, just harmless little girls. They drew carefully ruled lines to make the words behave on the page, clumsy and misspelled with their little kid hands. An unnamed anger and sadness welled up in him after reading their letters, making him irritable, acting out at dinner or picking a fight with someone before bed. He remembered when the girls would play school at the dining room table, copying words they couldn't understand from the encyclopedia. They called to him as he walked by, "Does this say something, is this a word?" He usually kept going, spelling swear words back at them and laughing on his way out the door.

They were a background for him, an essential given in his memory of his childhood, their blond heads forgotten even as they were seen. He teased the oldest girl relentlessly just to get a rise out of her but knew that he could count on her to not say anything important to any grown ups, especially their father. She helped him out once when he ran away from the house on Santa Lucia Street, a small flat roofed three-bedroom house in a subdivision across from a shopping mall.

He caught up with her as she walked home from school one afternoon and asked her to get him some food and a sleeping bag from their house. They both knew she would do it, even though she risked the wrath of Buckaflap. She whined and told him she didn't want to do it. When she went back to their house she looked for food that wouldn't be missed to take for him, quietly pulling a sleeping bag out of the messy camping closet, fairly sure their father wouldn't even know it was gone.

She walked to the end of their subdivision to a small farmer's field and a creek bed near by, where all the teens in the neighborhood hung out and smoked cigarettes. As she gave him the things he asked for he said thanks and called her little rat, the nickname he gave her when she told on him when they were younger, calling her by the old insult showing her he was still the big brother who could mess with her head. She flipped him off and walked back home.

Dear son,

I will be up to see you on Sunday. I will be bringing everyone. Do you want a radio that plugs into the wall outlet or one that works off battery?

I have not written because I did too much getting moved from our house and I have been ill.

When does school start for you?

I gave you the wrong address for our apartment. The correct address is:

1810 Monument Blvd. Apt. C-7
Concord, Calif. 94520

Love,
Dad
P.S. One dollar for you. Dad

Their father decided somewhere along the way that the middle brother liked radios but, really, he was the one who liked them. The middle brother might have feigned interest in the rare moments of wobbly cooperation and peace between them, a thin circling thread opening up above both their heads, silvery and invisible, fragile as tracing paper. He might have scoffed when he read of the offer of a radio but he would take it, he would take anything anyone would give him. He had few possessions at Hanna Boys Center and couldn't afford to be picky due to a grudge with Buckaflap. There was always the possibility of selling the radio or trading it for something with one of the other boys at the home.

Reading letters from Buckaflap was an exercise in irritation. The middle brother did not care that his father felt ill from moving, he deserved it. He felt no compassion for their father who just decided to give up their house with its fruit trees and secret spaces, its well-worn wooden floors, every grain and pattern innately known to all of them. The last straw in the letter, a close second after the fact that his father didn't even manage to send the right address of the new apartment where there was no room for him, was the single dollar bill that he included in the letter. Even their old English grandmother gave them a five-dollar bill for their birthdays, slipped inside a glittery card from Walgreens, signed in her spidery script.

A single dollar could mean a lot of things, its interpretation fluid and polarizing at the same time. It could be a slap in the face, meant to insult the person: here, you have little or no value, I am tossing this to you,

you are an afterthought like this crumpled bill and deserve nothing more. Or it could be more of a passive-aggressive move, indicating how selfless the impoverished giver was but he managed to part with a dollar while wearing his hair shirt, size extra large. Either way, the middle brother boiled, spending it as quickly as he could at the Hanna Boys Center's small general store.

Dear D,

Hi! I hope things are going well for you. The last time we met I told you I would introduce you to your new social worker. Her name Mrs. Carla Gato. Mrs. Gato and I will be coming up to see you on Tuesday November 18th.

See you then.

Sincerely,

Mr. Papo

The middle brother could not remember how many times he had been arrested. He tried to keep track at first, but after a while they all slipped into a hazy trail of police station processing and the inevitable phone call to Buckaflap. When his father arrived at the police station or juvenile hall to pick him up, he was usually clipped and surly with the officers, which the middle brother enjoyed, secretly relishing the haranguing insults from Buckaflap to whatever unfortunate officer was on duty. But once they were in the car, Buckaflap launched into one of two tirades. There was the tirade of what a mess he was making of his life and how he would never amount to anything if he kept this up. Or, he chose a stony angry silence, his wrath a three-dimensional poisonous gas pushing all the usable air out of the car. Sometimes Buckaflap left the middle brother in juvenile hall overnight if he could, or waited until the last possible moment to pick him up.

Mr. Papo was the social worker assigned to the middle brother due to all his police interactions and countless arrests. He would come over to their house every other week before the middle brother was sent to Hanna Boys Center. He sat on the couch asking awkward questions and ignoring the middle brother's sullen monosyllabic answers. Mr. Papo wore light colored cotton men's shirts rolled up at the elbow, sometimes with a tie or a shapeless sweater. At first the girls stayed and watched the interaction but quickly learned that Mr. Papo was a nosey man who could get their brother in serious trouble or even possibly get them all sent away to foster care. After that they slipped into their bedroom when he arrived, or snuck off to the back porch and played jail, pretending they were in jail or going to court with an inept social worker.

Mrs. Gato, the next social worker assigned to their family stayed with them for a long time, following them and visiting once a month long after the middle brother went to Hanna Boys Center. They didn't mind her as much. She was sharper than Mr. Papo but in a good way. She got food stamps for them and free school lunches. She was a huge woman who filled much of the couch, often surrounded by laundry. She would ask them why they didn't fold the laundry; didn't they see it there on the couch? Why didn't they help out around the apartment; did they think they were special? She was funny sometimes and she did things for them, so she earned her right to harass them. They wanted to be good when she was around. After many years of trying to help them she quit. It is not clear if she quit them or if she retired.

WITNESS

The police report consisted of three pages, all with carbon copies, the kind that had an inky back page that would make a copy of the witness's statement if they pressed hard enough with the pen. They smelled faintly like the dittos from grade school, handed out by teachers, sometimes still warm with that slightly sweet but sickening smell.

A generic police report has several blanks to be filled in at the top and then a large blank space on the bottom half of the page for the witness's statement. One of the blanks to be filled was for the type of complaint being investigated. The police report for the incident regarding the middle brother that night in the bar said *Attempted Murder*. In each of the five or six reports taken from the suspects in the bar that afternoon the complaint box was filled with the same two words, *Attempted Murder*, the words popping into the brain like a hot stray spark from a match or a drop of painful liquid, burning more as you tried to rub it away.

The middle brother and his friend John were drinking in a bar in Oakland and playing pool. They were both chronically under-employed. It was late afternoon, still light out it said in one of the reports. John was small and wiry and quick to run his mouth, especially when he was with the middle brother who was over six feet tall and not afraid of a little altercation when necessary. It could be said that sometimes they both enjoyed a good bar fight, it got them riled up and gave a focus to the failure they tried not to feel about their lives, lingering just below the surface, needing lots of alcohol to keep it at bay. Neither of them had finished high school and although the middle brother was a good mechanic he had trouble with bosses and with getting up in the morning. They both enjoyed blaming someone else for the frequent failure of their half-baked, sure-fire plans, frequently birthed on a barstool. They had been friends for a long time, creating schemes, legal and not so legal, trying to get ahead on their terms.

They were drinking and watching a game of pool when a guy with a long ponytail and a white Giants tee shirt bumped John in the gut with his pool stick. Words immediately flew, especially from John's yippy Terrier dog mouth. His base line demeanor was short fused and ready to erupt at a moment's notice. His words sailed high up into the stale bar air, hitting the ceiling like startled birds. As they continued to argue, the man in the Giants shirt threw a punch at the middle brother who was standing up at this point in the argument and heading towards him, fists cocked. John continued to yell and insult the guy with the ponytail and his friends, confident that the middle brother would handle the situation. The middle brother fell back from the first punch and hit his head on some kind of sharp object, maybe the edge or foot of the pool table as he went down. He hit the floor, able to see the blackened indoor-outdoor carpeting beneath the pool table, filmy with dust and cigarette ashes, the dried scaly circles of spilled drinks, hardened like tiny frozen lakes on the carpet.

The middle brother got up from the floor rubbing the back of his head. He pulled his hand away and looked at it to see if there was any blood. There wasn't. At this point the bartender threw them out of the bar. They stood outside, continuing the argument out onto the street, until the police came and took everyone's statements and dispersed them into the late afternoon.

John and the middle brother went back to their house and decided to watch TV. They lived in a condemned house owned by an elderly woman. They had conned her into letting them live there while they 'restored' it for her. They promised to bring it up to code for her. The house was up on thick blocks of wood to replace the rotten foundation. The middle brother assured the woman he knew how to do foundation work. He went as far as to get the house up on the wood blocks so they could do the foundation work but somehow he and John had gone through the money the owner gave them without getting to the foundation to do the repairs.

While they watched TV the middle brother kept saying he had a headache and then he threw up a few times. They decided to go to the hospital to get him checked out. They headed to Highland Hospital to the emergency room, expecting to wait for several hours but were taken in immediately. The middle brother sat down on the gurney as the nurse took his vital signs. John sat in the orange plastic chair next to the door, watching the nurse, silent.

The middle brother said he was having trouble seeing

out of one eye and then suddenly hunched over and passed out on the gurney. John had to help the nurse catch him so the middle brother didn't fall onto the floor. A code blue was called and he was rushed away on the gurney. John stood in the hallway watching them roll the middle brother away. He started to cry. Turns out they were rushing him into to surgery as they thought he must have a brain bleed from the blow to the head and time was critical. The middle brother never regained consciousness.

He was in surgery for many hours. His friend John was kicked out of the triage room and sent back to the ER waiting room. He sat down and watched TV, not seeing or understanding anything on the screen. His heart was hammering in his chest. The fight kept replaying in torn bits of time in his head, sometimes focusing on the guy with the pool stick as he threw the first punch, his long black hair pulled back into a lame ponytail held in place in neatly spaced intervals with goofy black hair ties, the kind women wore when they worked out, or cleaned house, utilitarian, no nonsense black ties that did not slip, just did their job of keeping the hair where it should be.

Sometimes the flashback was the middle brother falling, again and again like a skipping film reel, his body disappearing behind the pool table as he fell. Or sometimes it was to the horrible image of the middle brother beginning to fall off the gurney as he lost consciousness. This was the worst fragment of all. His best friend suddenly lifeless in the tiny room, a large silent amphibian attempting to slip off the gurney and back into the sea, with only gravity in play, every other bodily function gone, switched over to another frequency, the middle brother's brain now unknowable.

From the small orange chair where John sat waiting that first night, he must have known that everything had just utterly changed for both of them, John's mouth the cause of all of it. John desperately wanted to find the guys who did this to his friend but he was powerless to do anything without the middle brother. Alone he'd get his ass beat for sure. He was a tiny yappy dog without his front man. John stood up suddenly and left the waiting room to go call the middle brother's sister who lived near by and who sometimes slept with him. She would know what to do. She would call everyone to come.

WAITING

After many hours in surgery the middle brother was moved to the intensive care unit of Highland Hospital, one of the best ICU's in the state for trauma. This kind of statistic was meant to be comforting for those loved ones once removed, listening on the other end of the telephone, hearing, not living the harrowing details couched in medical jargon just learned, their gravely ill loved ones providing a crash course in hospital speak.

After the surgery the middle brother was put on a ventilator. A thick plastic tube ran down into his throat, carefully placed into his lungs, breathing for him in measured amounts, the air being forced out of his lungs on the exhale, in on the inhale. His mechanical breath sometimes made a small whooshing sound, sometimes it sounded like a sigh that startled them with its humanness. Then they would quickly look at him, hoping this was the TV moment when he would wake up and life could return to itself, the messy middle brother narrowly escaping another close call.

The parking lot of Highland Hospital was sad and beat. Fast food litter laced the bottom edges of the chain link fence, tossed cigarette butts and thick raised oil spots bulged up on the few empty parking places. The entrance to the hospital was highly secured, two security guards flanking each set of large glass doors outside, then two more in the lobby, one standing just inside the door and one sitting at some kind of ledger behind a thick plexiglass window. The guard's stiff demeanor told each visitor he knew who was lying and who was about to cause trouble. He did not greet people who approached his window, instead raised his head up and a little to the side with no eye contact, suspicion like tiny invisible bees buzzing above his head.

The breathing tube from the ventilator was secured with flesh colored tape at the corner of the middle brother's mouth. It looked like a giant clown straw hanging out of his mouth, or a strange cartoon-like smoking pipe. None of the siblings could go there and make the obvious joke the middle brother might have appreciated, flipping them off in acknowledgement of the attempt with his bent middle finger.

His head was thickly bandaged with white frothy gauze, his head shaved beneath it. When the siblings were finally allowed in to see him after the surgery, they were allowed to see him in fifteen-minute increments, taking turns, two at a time. They always checked for new blood on the bandages then quickly looked away, returning to scanning his impassive face, landing always back on his eyes, which remained shut. His body lay still in the hospital bed in what looked like a deep sleep or some state resembling sleep. The hospital gown was dwarfed on his giant body, his dark chest hair popping out the top of the edge of the hospital gown, *Highland Hospital* printed at evenly spaced intervals on the faded fabric. In one of his hands was an IV taped down and dated in someone's tiny handwriting, clear liquid going somewhere into his stilled frame, hydrating and lubricating his body in hopes of pleasing the brain into waking up.

The middle brother's brain, once a closed system like some kind of futuristic ecosphere, had been violated more than once. The impact when he fell to the floor in the bar the first insult, the swiftness of the fall, his weight and height and gravity all amounting to a rupture in this ecosystem. The boney skull was designed to avoid such insults, but only up to a certain point. Velocity and angle and impact a physiology of physics culminating in a broken and bleeding vessel in the closed world of his brain. His skull was a good one, large and thick, the fused over suture lines like fossilized riverbeds, evidence of his birth, the squeeze so tight his infant head was born soft and pliant, movable bones fusing quickly in the first weeks of his life.

The second violation was the surgery late that first night. The surgeons carefully cutting into the middle brother's skull, their many years of grueling training humbling and irritating in its constant reminder to be careful, a litany to all who enter into the brain that they must be very careful, any slip or uncertain touch reminding them of their insignificance when it comes to investigating the spheres of the brain. The reminder of how little the strange domain they were entering with their knives and their scalpels was understood, and how quickly irreparable damage could be done to its blind allies which gave away little, withholding information that many a surgeon took personally as they studied harder and worked harder to breech the mysterious secrets of the brain.

A stay in the intensive care unit is an elite invitation. To be allowed to stay there is evaluated every morning by a team of doctors and nurses, making their decision like a secret society, a cluster of white coats and hospital scrubs scanning the medical chart from the night before to determine who would be staying for another twenty-four hours and who was stable enough to go elsewhere. The machine encircled beds of the ICU in high demand always, gunshot wounds and car crashes and other life-threatening daily trauma clamoring to be let in, to be given a bed in the unit.

The next two weeks at Highland evolved into a surreal routine, the sibling visits an invisible pattern forming as they stayed close to the middle brother's sleeping body as much as their worlds would allow them. They came in shifts, the oldest brother visiting every morning, watching and waiting for the middle brother to return to his body. The youngest brother came by almost every day as well. He delivered auto parts so he showed up in the late afternoon after his deliveries were done. He was mostly silent, a mass of love and fear sitting next to the hospital bed, glaring at the machines that were helping the middle brother breathe.

The oldest sister came mostly on the weekend. She had two small children and had to feed them dinner and bathe them and put them to bed, trying not to picture her brother's tall motionless body and the huge bandage on his head as she went through the motions with her kids. The youngest sister came most days as well. She drove a school bus so she was finished worked in the early afternoon. She and the youngest brother often sat together silently. Staring but not seeing the strange machines keeping their brother alive.

They grew accustomed to the security guards gruffness and the occasional drama in the lobby as families cried and fought and blamed each other, a physical enactment of the fear and love they held in their bodies, erupting like a geyser only just discovered, baffling and wild as it made its presence known, raw and substantial on the cold tiled floors of the waiting room.

They even got used to the horrible and unchanging vision of the middle brother lying silently in the hospital bed that moved in various tilts, inflating like clockwork to pad the weight of his inert body, his giant limbs bent like the fallen wings of a bird of prey, stilled in the bed. His head remained bandaged, traces of new hair growing where it had been shaved for the surgery emerging beneath the bandage. The ventilator remained, humming and whirring next to his bed, the tube down his throat and the constant noise a reminder of what was needed to keep him alive in that bed, waiting for change, anything at all to be the turn in the road.

After a few stable days the doctors told them that the middle brother needed a tracheostomy. They needed to cut a hole in their brother's throat for a more permanent placement of the ventilator tube keeping him alive. The doctors presented it to them like it was an option, a decision they had to make as his family, consent a formality that felt like falling for the unlucky sibling who was at the bedside that day and had to make the call.

He got the tracheostomy and now they could see his whole face, his mouth that remained half closed, his beard growing, the encroaching stubble that kept on happening while his brain was on silent was baffling. Someone was shaving him, an unseen nurse or nurse's aide was touching his mute skin, washing his face, his body, turning him every few hours to prevent bedsores. Sometimes they must have spoken to him as they cared for him, telling him what they were doing when they did the medical things they needed to do. Sometimes they said hello quietly as they did their work on his body.

The plan was to let the middle brother stabilize, to allow his body to try to heal from the 'insult,' they called it, and the surgery. The doctors talked about swelling a lot. The swelling in his brain was a problem even after they released the tension of the bleed in his head. The swelling was a part of his unresponsiveness and only time would tell if there would ever be any real change in his condition. The swelling became an evil force in their minds, an unseen enemy that moved slowly, if at all, giving little ground in the land of his brain.

So, they waited, rotating their lives to be at Highland, as the middle brother 'stabilized,' according to the ICU team. His ventilator settings were stable, he didn't have a fever and his blood work looked fine. He was just still on life support, unable to breathe on his own, in a coma, needing constant nursing care around the clock and could do nothing for himself. The word *stable* took on a new meaning in the sanitized hospital room of the ICU, stable like a boulder poised on a cliff, stable like waiting for the wind to make up its mind where to land its offshore hurricane force, picking up houses and trees as it comes to roost, waiting for the rain and its inevitable flooding.

The team felt he was ready to go to a skilled nursing

facility. The siblings were afraid of leaving the safety of Highland Hospital and the ICU. The idea of a nursing home did not foster hope in any of their minds. To them it meant decay and neglect filtered through an ever-present smell of urine. The Highland doctors had done everything they could for him but to the siblings he looked basically the same as when he arrived, a giant sleeping man with a head bandaged in miles of gauze, surrounded by machines and people and still oblivious to it all. The longer he was unresponsive, the bleaker his prospects were for waking up. Even the siblings could sense that but would never say it. They were torn between giving him time for a miracle and freeing him from his broken body.

When the doctors decided he was ready to leave the ICU they did not mince words with the siblings. The attending physician summarized it in a bedside meeting with them, "He has sustained a massive assault to his brain and the information gathered from the scans and tests and various evaluations has led us believe there are very few options. He will probably never wake up and the longer he is asleep the worse the likelihood there is of any kind of survival off of life support."

He paused and looked at the siblings and then rested his eyes on something somewhere over their heads. "The options are to take him off life support now or to wait another few months and revaluate then, at which time I honestly don't think there will be any significant change. You are free to wait a while, if that is what the family needs to do."

They had a meeting with the Highland social worker, the siblings leery and battle-scarred from the Mr. Papos' and the Mrs. Gatos' from their childhood who wanted to help, who were paid to help, and who somehow always got it wrong. All four siblings were at the meeting, presenting a united hostile front. Their father was dead by this time so they were it, the family unit, the ball of genetic hints and clues, hands and fingers spooky in their echoing identical shapes, jaw lines and brows so similar as to be unseen. The similarities blew forth into shaky consciousness with their repetition, molded from the original connecting mass, unbroken even as the damage lay at their feet. They were called together, for him, lying in the hospital bed, silent as a cell begging to cross the membrane of their bigger body.

The middle brother was to be moved to Fairmont, a small skilled nursing facility in Hayward. He would be moved by ambulance the next day if they were okay with the plan. They were in theory, but the suddenness of the move felt like they were being thrown out of the safety of the ICU. The youngest brother did not want to wait six months but he kept silent. At the time he didn't understand that the ventilator was keeping his brother alive. He thought that if the middle brother could just be given a break from all the technology, maybe he would breathe and wake up on his own. They just needed to give him a chance.

He could not stop thinking about the last thing he said to the middle brother who was blowing him off once again to go drink at the bar with John, "You'd rather drink than help us, your own family," he'd said.

Even though the middle brother did seem to live in that bar, the youngest brother could not bear the idea of that being the last thing he had said to the middle brother. He dove down deep into a hole of guilt, a tunneling lined with dark wet tears, a scratchy eyed sadness, self-inflicted arrows of judgment, never sated, a thin line of logic fighting in the space where sleep might come. He just wanted the middle brother to wake up, to be alive and go to the bar everyday if that was the price for him to come back. He didn't want to wait, he wanted him free, sure that he would open his eyes if he just had some unfettered space.

They decided to give him six months, a solid chunk of time, a more than generous chunk of time for the invisible swelling to morph and dissipate, to help make the path known to him, and to them. They knew any sort of time line was arbitrary, the long end of a hunch and an obligation to his body and to their sibling body, unspeakably harmed, the answer already in their lungs, waiting to be the last breath.

FAIRMONT

One of the respiratory therapists at Fairmont who took care of the middle brother owned a Dodge Valiant. It was white and had been fully restored. The tires had chrome rims with red around the edges, baby moons they were called. The body of the car was smooth and immaculate and pointy in all the right places. The sisters could see the push button transmission on the column as they peered into the car windows, hands against the glass to prevent the glare, examining the interior of the car in disbelief and awe. The car felt like a good omen to them, its exact message never coming clear, but the connection to the middle brother seemed unmistakable.

The middle brother's Valiant was light blue, the older model with the sloped window in the back. It was actually his car, not one of the many he stole just to steal them, the strange enjoyment he found in moving someone's car from place to place, taking a ride like some kind of cruel chess game, his move launching a threat to their sanity that made him laugh out loud when he pictured them finding, or not finding their car where they were sure they had left it.

He always said he bought the Valiant for one hundred dollars from an 'acquaintance,' someone from his subterranean world of cars and dark garages and afternoon drinking. They assumed he got it from one of those men, like him, who gathered and talked of elaborate plans and great ideas routinely formulated in a dim bar in the middle of the day.

The middle brother's Valiant had a thin chrome line around the sloped back window and along the sides of the body of the car, creating a slight ridge in the curve of the doors. It was a husk of a car really. The vinyl seats deflated and split in many places, the body dinged and scraped almost completely, rust feathering out from beneath the car, silently creeping over the sharp edges of the rear fenders where the tiny red back up lights still shone in the dark.

Its interior, though ripped and worn, was red. There was a huge red steering wheel laced with chrome circles and a push button transmission on the column that he pointed out repeatedly with child-like excitement to any one he showed the car. It was as though he had a brand-new Cadillac; the enormity of actually owning something an intangible that he was finally part of.

The two sisters picked up where they left off during the months spent at Highland sitting with the middle brother. They hadn't a falling out so much as their lives had taken different turns. The oldest had two small children and worked nights as a nurse. Her marriage was on its last legs, and she was always tired. The youngest was a loner by nature, rarely had boyfriends, and if she did they were usually friends of the middle brother and so were often flaky and a continual source of disappointment.

The old comfort and ease of being together plumped itself back to life in the filtered hospital air. They had a way of talking and gesturing that was their own sub-language, nothing elaborate or forcefully created, rather a natural out cropping, laced with the intimately shared years of their childhood spent close as twins in a house of boys.

When the middle brother was moved to Fairmont the girls arranged their schedules to visit him together every week. They usually met in the parking lot, gathering courage from each other as they headed into to see the 'sleeping' middle brother, his dark hair growing back in, starting to cover the large C shaped incision on the side of his head. It seemed to be a fairly decent nursing home, their gauge being the lack of urine smell when they walked into the lobby. The staff were busy, often preoccupied, walking briskly past the doorway, disappearing into rooms, speaking to them only when they tracked one of them down to ask a question.

They usually arrived at about eleven a.m. That way the morning care was done and the mistakes of the night before were righted, messes cleaned up and beds changed. One week they arrived earlier and didn't call ahead. The nurses appeared irritated and even a little nervous when they saw the sisters, fake scolding them for not calling first.

When they went into the middle brother's room, he was uncovered, his hospital gown hiked up around his waist, his adult diaper looked heavy with urine. His face was unshaven, and his fingernails were long and claw like. They looked for his nurse and told her their brother needed to be changed and they would come back when she had cleaned him up. Shaken, they headed to the cafeteria to wait. For once they were silent as they walked down the covered hallway to the cafeteria. They desperately needed the illusion that he was in a good place, that he was somewhere where the people were taking at least adequate care of his inert body. He was one of the limbs on their tree, not just a drunk who fought in bars, giving away his precious life, felled onto a grimy floor underneath a pool table.

They learned a lot about nursing home life and called ahead religiously after that day. Some days he looked more cared for than others. They could tell when whomever had him as a patient on a particular day either did or didn't have the time or inclination to really wash his skin, now slightly sallow and waxy. They could see if the caretaker took the time to shave him and his cut nails. The staff left the mark of their level of compassion like a signature on his body.

The sisters found each other again at Fairmont, standing on each side of the middle brother's bed, occasionally holding his stiff hand or touching his hair as they talked. They rambled through their childhood, through the events leading up to the accident, blasting and condemning John, whom they decided was the one who didn't deserve his own life. They submerged themselves into the bond they had always had as sisters, one that allowed for love and humor, uncertainty and loneliness. They wordlessly understood the shared sense of having endured a childhood of constant uncertainty and scarcity, finding an early safety in each other, loyalty, envy, love and anger, all melded into their sister skin, beginning in the bunk-beds of their childhood, a safety and an acceptance of each other, solid when almost nothing else was.

They talked a lot about the bar fight and John and the unknown man who had punched the middle brother. They needed to find a place to put the anguish of waiting for what they knew was the end of his life, and they wanted justice. They wanted the guy who did this to their brother to pay, to be arrested and brought to trial. If they couldn't find him, then they wanted John to pay, his head on a platter still not an even exchange for their brother's now useless life.

Being of the TV generation of the seventies the sisters decided to sleuth a little on their own TV shows like *Hawaii Five-O* and *Adam-12* giving them imaginary skills they thought they could use to find the nameless man with the long ponytail who punched the middle brother. They went to the bar where the fight happened, it looked harmless and small and sad in the early afternoon light. They talked to the bartender who replied in small grunts of sound to all their questions, his face impassive, his eyes landing on their faces only when absolutely necessary, even after they told him that the middle brother was now languishing in a hospital bed on a ventilator after a fight in his bar.

This approach did not get the result they wanted, the opposite occurred, the bartender may have felt guilty by proxy or was afraid of the possibility of trouble with the police at the very least. He became busy with the ice machine at the far end of the bar, ducking his head below the bar while they stood there. After taking a quick and disappointing walk around the pool table, the sisters left, squinting back out in the sun. They were flattened at the dead end they so quickly touched, the first of many to come.

The older sister suggested they go to the middle brother's house, she wanted to see where he lived, she wanted to see if she could feel the thread of his disappearing life by being among his things, hoping to find missing pieces to his fallen life by standing in his kitchen. She was sure there must be a clue in his dresser drawers or in the kitchen cupboards.

The younger sister had remained close to the middle brother. They spoke on the phone regularly and she sometimes hung out with him and John, watching them drink and play cards. She slept with John sometimes while disliking him for being who he was, a mouthy little man who did not think the rules of adult life applied to him, that the world owed him something for being born. She could not contort him into a nice man she could love no matter how many tries she gave him.

The younger sister tried to warn the older one, to prepare her for how the middle brother really lived his life, for what he was now, a man almost erased, existing under the radar. He and John lived in the condemned house of an old woman they had convinced to let them live in her house while 'remodeling' it. The money she gave them was gone and they had little to show for it, a looming deadline already come and gone.

Inside, the house was barren, there were minimal leftover furnishings, all with the greasy patina of old grime, the deflated contours of time passing. The kitchen was a large square room; there was an empty space where a kitchen table might have once been, shiny wood cabinets of knotty pine lined the two far walls. The older sister opened the refrigerator like an afterthought, a gesture of familiarity, of idle curiosity and familial permission. She expected beer, lots of it, but found only old condiments and not much else. She wondered out loud where his beer might be. The younger sister told her he had given beer up a long time ago, now he drank vodka, he said it was quicker.

Next they went to see the police detective assigned to the middle brother's case. His name was Detective Paniagua and he dressed in typical cop desk job attire, a short sleeve dress shirt, a polyester sports coat over the back of his chair. He wore black slacks and black pleather shoes. When he came out to meet them, he did not offer any condolences for the middle brother or offer to shake their hands. Instead he looked annoyed at their arrival and told them he probably wouldn't be much help to them as the DA frowned on bar fights, shrugging his shoulders in the resulting silence.

The sisters, stunned by his bluntness, still hoped the detective might be an ally if they could let him see how brutally wounded the middle brother was. They asked him a litany of naïve questions, had he talked to John, had they found the man with the ponytail, did they question the people who worked at the bar, had they brought anyone in? Detective Paniagua, held up his hands and started talking over them, "The department is doing everything they can but your brother was in a bar fight and the DA frowns on bar room brawls, so. . ."

The detective looked at them beneath scratchy black eye brows, the corners of his mouth curled and pinched, judgment coming off his face, folding his fleshy cheeks into two pear shaped jowls.

The girls were deflated once again in their efforts to

find justice for the middle brother, calling the cranky detective "Detective Pantywaist" as they walked to the car. They were out of their element with the police and the criminal justice system, stepping into the land of perps and DAs who were all powerful, their mere frown putting a stop to an investigation of a possible murder deemed not important because drunken incidents occurred all too often. Violence wicked with the flame of alcohol burning hot and fast, jumping any kind of boundary thrown in its path, until it burned itself and everything around it down to the blackened ground.

The oldest girl called an acquaintance who was a lawyer and he too offered little hope for the middle brother due to the 'nature of the crime.' They began to see that justice truly was bought and paid for and they didn't have the funds to be in the game. The older girl took to saying that if the middle brother were a Kennedy the man with the ponytail would be arrested and on trial. They reluctantly gave up their efforts to find someone to take responsibility for the harm done to the middle brother, his death on pause, waiting for the rest of his siblings to catch up to him.

HOSPICE

After the allotted six months passed and the middle brother's condition was still unchanged, they knew it was time to make a decision and have a family meeting with the Fairmont social worker. The time they had given themselves to wait for the middle brother to breathe on his own, the time to give them even the smallest sign of hope, was over. At the beginning of the waiting period six months felt far away, a vague point in someone else's future. The burden of visiting him, showing up week after week, bringing their love and their loyalty into the hospital room, their false cheer and pretend conversations with him were tinged with a bleakness and a growing sense of bodily panic they hid from in their waking hours. To wait for him was a push to some forever moment that had no reward, the only point of movement the time they allotted themselves and his borrowed breath, pushed into him and pulled out by the humming machine at the side of his bed.

It was the oldest brother who started the conversation with the rest of them. By this time their visits to the middle brother were a part of all their lives, the passage of time the only thing changing. The six-month mark was both a relief and a giving up that none of them wanted once it arrived. They were scared to let him go and scared to keep him in his crumpled body, afraid to see that he was dead already, and afraid to see him linger if they were wrong. And they were angry that they had to be the ones to make the choice-less last choice for him.

The four siblings gathered around a large table in a Fairmont conference room, weary and resigned, no one speaking as they waited for the social worker to come in. When the social worker arrived, she spoke carefully, avoiding words like *die* or *death*, skirting them like dark holes she had to maneuver to keep her own life safe. She asked each of the siblings around the table to speak, to voice what they wanted for the middle brother who no longer formed words. It was a hearing on whether a tree was allowed to fall or a bird shot from the sky could drop, no logic, the mind unable to cobble the fit of dying, the husk of their brother lying in the other wing of the nursing home still and always waiting.

Each sibling voted to take the middle brother off life support, their unanimity a last act of love making it hard for them to breath, their own lungs pink and capable, the colors in the day suddenly more vivid, the blues and greens, outlines not usually visible, illuminating the day that still went on, cars on the freeway, a honking in the distance not stopping as they decided to stop him.

The social worker quickly ended the meeting as she felt their painful resolve, giving them the details they would need to proceed. They gathered outside the conference room after the meeting and planned between themselves a schedule of who would sit with the middle brother until he passed. The oldest girl took the first night, the oldest brother the second, the youngest brother the night after that. They didn't know how long it would take but they cleared their calendars one last time for the middle brother, taking their turn to show up and sit with him before he went away for good.

The middle brother re-emerged a little, looking more like himself without all the tubes and machines attached to him. His body was still most of the time, except for an occasional shudder of breath or the jerky repetitive movement he made with his shoulders or the grinding of his teeth, the scary stray movements lost signals emitting from deep within his broken brain.

The hospice room was small, just his bed and two chairs, a nurse looking in on him from time to time on the first day. There was a quiet in the room, the light and the voices of those who came and went was softer. The air in the room held a revered waiting of the approaching finality of the end of a life, the inert last part of the middle brother's life, a small honored waiting held in the sparse room, his imminent death transfixing the physical space. The noise and the battle of his body nearly gone, the spin of the globe pushing his life energy elsewhere, creating a small necessary stillness, a suspended state of allowing, a state of no resistance, its soft current seeping into those who were near, those consenting to be part of the humble, holy, horrible moment, when the arc of the heart driven light lifts, energy leaving yet another human, the body shed, unknowingly gifted in its very occurrence, the mystery that is consciousness a wild pony running away, cold air pushing out its nostrils in a cloud of white as it runs up a canyon and out of reach, for now.

The middle brother died the second day. The oldest

brother arriving exactly at eight a.m. to relieve his sister who had spent a sleepless night watching the middle brother through longer and longer moments of stillness interrupted by small frantic bucking movements from his body. The oldest brother was a tall man, slightly ducking his head as he entered the room out of habit and the muscle memory of grazing his head many a time on irregular doorways.

A nurse came in shortly after eight that morning, her quiet body only slightly swirling the air in the tiny room, her energy a gentle, minimal presence. She looked at the middle brother, a giant grounded crane occasionally lurching in his last captivity, then she looked at the oldest brother who dissolved into tears as he felt her glance. She made a quiet humming noise in the back of her throat and guided him without touching him to sit in the chair.

They sat together in the room that morning with the middle brother, the nurse occasionally adjusting something for the middle brother, setting free a twisted blanket, putting chapstick on his craggy lips. The oldest brother sat silently in the chair, his mind a whirring wheel of fragments of memories of the middle brother. His life a country in their sibling globe, his arms and legs the territories within, cities, states, and smooth fields, blood the rivers feeding their earth, ground forced mountains a protoplasm of sameness, their essence in its dirt, lifted in the rain, marked in the dawn, indelible in their bones extending with the identical shape in their fingers.

He died that morning. The oldest brother sat motionless in the hard, plastic chair next to his bed, watching as the oxygen in the air failed to push its way through the middle brother's body any longer. The color of his skin slowly cooling into the dark blue surface of a ruddy alpine lake, the coming cold rippling the surface as it landed, its new season now here, taking the color from his skin, a leaf falling off the tree.

THE GUN

The idea of getting a gun swam into the oldest brother's consciousness for the first time at Highland Hospital, when every visit to see the middle brother was a shock to his own body, seeing the middle brother bandaged and silent, the ventilator there like an unwanted intruder, humming its veracity, unaffected by the torrent of disbelief of those coming and going, shock silencing them as they stood at his bedside.

The oldest brother was an outlier in their family, putting himself through UC Berkeley and learning to fly airplanes when he was only eighteen. He turned some imaginary luminous corner in his teen years into the straight life, as he and the middle brother called it, and the middle brother did not follow him. The oldest brother started to work for money instead of stealing it from the tidy houses in their neighborhood or robbing the local businesses.

He eventually had his own business as an electrical engineer, morphing into a tall confident man in a sports jacket with a solid handshake and a clear gaze. He worked hard to escape the memories of the Hamburger Helper bought with food stamps and the searing eyes of the grown ups boxing him into their prediction of failure for their family, its stink coming off his body and his family name, dirtying the air of their gaze.

He truly believed, before the accident, that hard work was the only necessity in the equation for success and he was going to be a part of its calculus, his childhood crimes relegated to the back country, a craggy territory of a different time. His progress—his successes—a three-dimensional relief, a proof he needed mostly for himself. He liked his orchestrated life now: a wife and two children and a house in the suburbs, his desire for safety and escape sated in the three-bedroom floor plan and two car garage that held his wife's Datsun 280Z with a custom license plate, 'Elegance is Everything.' He lived in a planned subdivision in Fremont, all of the circular streets named after different kinds of wine. He lived on Merlot Street, which he pronounced Mer-lot Street.

The oldest brother had also gone to see the DA about the middle brother's case. Maybe he thought reason and logic would prevail, man to man. He imagined he and the DA discussing the case and agreeing about what seemed so clear to the oldest brother. His brother was in a vegetative state due to a blow to the head from a guy with a long black ponytail, whose name and where abouts the police knew from the police report that the man with the long ponytail filled out himself. Bring him in and prosecute him, done.

But the DA did not share his point of view. The DA lived in the world of the law. He spoke its language and knew the twists and turns of due process. The DA said there was not enough evidence: "He's not dead," he told the oldest brother.

The oldest brother bought a .38 revolver and a box of bullets from a gun store in San Jose. There was a ten-day waiting period and a background check, which he passed easily as his crimes from childhood were sealed and in his adult life he was a perfect law-abiding citizen. He had experience with BB guns as a kid, shooting them with the middle brother at birds and cans and occasionally each other, always aiming for the butt or lower extremities.

He once stole a gun he found in a house he had broken into. It was a .22 black revolver. At the time he just wanted to possess it, to feel what a gun felt like in his hands, the weight and the cool metal silent, its abilities hidden in the barrel, the trigger, the blast and its inevitable damage when released into the unsuspecting air. He kept the gun for three days, carefully hiding it from the middle brother. Then he took it apart and buried the parts in several different places on Shell Ridge, the hilly land at the edge of the neighborhood where they had played as children.

The oldest brother drove by the bar where the 'incident' took place many times, sometimes going inside, looking for the man with the long ponytail, the gun in his car, needing only his decision. The eldest brother waited for a sighting of the man with the ponytail, who got to walk freely, eating and sleeping, fighting and drinking while the middle brother lay silenced in a hospital bed. He never saw him.

The injustice of his brother's life, the unfairness of his brother's injury hurt his engineer brain, trained in logic and problem solving. There was no linear progression, no solution to be found if he just did things in the right order.

Any formula he tried to apply did not fit the destroyed body of his brother now perpetually in a hospital gown, insect limbs stiff with disuse and the inertia of his brain. He could not find a way to hold the damage he saw day after day, the echoing memory of his brother before the fight rang loud in his brain. He had always tried to help the middle brother out, someone who often did not want his help. Their adult relationship bumpy, the middle brother calling the oldest brother a goody-goody with his big job and his house in the suburbs, a new bitterness forming with each of the oldest brother's successes.

When the DA said there wasn't enough evidence, that the middle brother wasn't dead, something dark shifted in the oldest brother. He fell back into his primitive brain, back into the boy from Walnut Blvd who was fearless and hungry, the boy who would do anything, steal anything, destroy that which harmed him, taking anything and everything because no one cared about him or his siblings, so fuck it. A cold power sloughing off into his hands from the things he stole, the harm he inflicted. The idea of the gun blossomed there, vining its way into his every waking moment. He felt himself becoming justified, righteous even, in his mission.

In the beginning he drove to the bar when he couldn't stand how he felt, the bubbles of hate hot in his brain. While his children slept snug in their beds, the rage and sorrow built in his limbs, the blackness of his thoughts a pain he could not bear. He sometimes drove to the bar several times a week in those six months of waiting, walking in circles around the pool table, wanting something to manifest and change in the pilly green felt, something to lift the bone deep ache of his brother's stopped life.

Following the law was a cruel joke, a useless map to somewhere nonexistent, a point off the horizon with old wooden ships and sepia sails falling off the edge, a dragon's tail with a Poseidon tip coaxing and repelling those who look too long. The law's protection was meant for other people, those other more deserving people who had two parents and warm houses and hot food. The oldest brother had spent his entire life struggling, sure that the world had something he did not, laboring under the weight of forced entry into that other world he thought he could master if only he did what they did.

The oldest brother put himself through college and did well, he flew airplanes and paid his taxes and made money, lots of it for awhile, yet he knew in the muted, inaudible region of his forgotten island, his origin was volcanically joined, linked forever just below the surface with the rest of his sibling tribe, that he would always be with them, the motherless boy looking in the windows of those who had more.

It was a bright morning outside, clocks moving their arms forward, digital numbers flipping the seconds forward. It was the middle of the week and his brother was dead, had in fact just died that very moment. He stepped out of the hospice room and looked outside without seeing the hospital's sad landscaping. The uniform green hedges that never grew and never died, Poinsettia trees with their thin branches and wane red leaf like flowers lining the sidewalk. He did not know what to do, panic rising in his body, his existence without his brother a waterline quickly vanishing, his eyes breathing tears, the salty beads a white burning roar of the indelible image of his brother's changing color, his mother's soft smile floating and falling as it disappeared with the middle brother, drifting in a river swollen with leaving, pulling his life to its known edge, nothing left to grasp onto on its bare muddy banks. Cars still rolling by on the freeway, voices in the air fuzzed and incomprehensible. He was alone.

He called everyone, unprepared for the renewal of piercing pain each time he had to repeat the words to each of them, the pain of feeling them crumble as they received the news of the middle brother's death, physically inevitable, predicted absolutely but traumatizing anyway in its formal arrival. They were stunned on the other end of the phone, the youngest girl sobbing as soon as she heard the oldest brother's voice.

The middle brother's death was a severing, a vital something torn away from them, one of their own gone, a limb of their tribe no longer standing, his nameless island slipping back into the sea, folded into the cloudy bottom of the ocean floor in its soundless descent.

The youngest brother was silent on the phone, receding back into the filmy safety of his habitual cave of silence. He was not able to speak, his muteness mistaken for indifference by some, by those who did not know the power of silence or of its cunning hold, gripping its captives in a sticky web of all things unspoken, so hard to breach, while the remaining feelings gather in the body, bulging with the increasing pressure. He was captive to the practice of silence and its dark companion, food, chips and soda, and more, the balm their father had taught them long ago.

They were all relieved in a confusing way. It was a best of the worst-case scenario that he had died so quickly. It made them feel like they made the right decision for him, their unspoken fear that he would languish for weeks or even longer by their hand unbearable to imagine. It was also a stark and undeniable physical truth of the profound harm that had been done to him that night in the bar. He probably would have died at Highland months ago if they had made the choice then. He was dead then and he was dead now, six months later, the man with the ponytail a murderer.

They knew they had done everything they could for him, from the very first moment, showing up and looking out for him, protecting him, a respect and love naturally coming forth from all of them as solid and as total as any 'real' family anywhere. They were present for him, not looking in from some window but in the room with him, of him, every step of the way. They had become the real family in the window, they had enough love and compassion and sustenance for all of them, they were there and they had done it right.

EPILOGUE

They were a formed whole all along, remaining so even when they scattered later on. The reminder of their shared past carrying a charge that was hard to sustain as it both pulled them and repelled them, the magnet of memory repolarizing the years they had spent together with their father and without her, their mother, her life their true home, the place of their true belonging.

They were a raw beautiful aggregate, a combine found in a hot yellow field, a rare quartz vein discovered in the plain sandstone hills, fossils in their arms and legs placed by their mother and father, and parts further on in time and place, England and Ireland and all parts north, cold and matter of factualized, but a total none the less, a completion that held its form, sheading silent tears when his part of them slipped away.

It is true that the first few years after their mother's death they lived in a kind of moonscape, populated by strangers who wanted to help, two-dimensional figures inhabiting their days, washing clothes and cooking love-less food, their father swallowed into the grief-blackened earth of her death. Their child minds told them that it must be their fault, just by being born they were tainted and had caused her to leave them. A child's merciless self-centered logic the only response to a tragedy they had no words for, leaving them to live a life they had no way of knowing was not in their control, a fairy tale cruelty bestowed on their tiny bodies, no spell to be broken or journey to return from, just their left over lives, the smudge of their mother's dark eyed glance on their foreheads.

The five of them were born into a smoldering landscape then, the youngest girl the one closest to the firing line, her birth the arrival of a fault line of cells and air and flesh and its falling blood, her mother gone in an instant just weeks after she was born while the living trees erupted green and brilliant from the charred hillsides of later on.

They grew up and grew apart, joking about the food stamps and the awful freeze-dried camping food when they got together. They laughed a lot, joking a habit of deflection, a shield each one of them learned to wield from their very first encounters with the world. Levity a weapon that kept them safe and far from the truth of the grief they were born into, staining their breath. Making jokes taught them how to run away in plain sight, how to hide behind the diluting pain of words, laughter their safety, making some of them oddities perhaps, but they didn't have to feel any of it with the protection of their flippancy, a wavery shell they discovered long ago from the bottom of their island sea.

The four of them were now the last of their shrinking chain of islands, time and weather the final determination of what stays anyway, of what is remembered, the present the only moment not a memory, fused with filmy perceptions, the small matter of their lives a layer in the turning earth, a speck, the old pain of their childhood a chronic burning sensation that none of them could ever really rid themselves, the safety of the returning winds the relief they sought to wait it out.

ABOUT ATMOSPHERE PRESS

Atmosphere Press is an independent, full-service publisher for excellent books in all genres and for all audiences. Learn more about what we do at atmospherepress.com.

We encourage you to check out some of Atmosphere's latest releases, which are available at Amazon.com and via order from your local bookstore:

Waking Up Marriage: Finding Truth In Your Partnership, nonfiction by Bill O'Herron

Eat to Lead, nonfiction by Luci Gabel

An Ambiguous Grief, a memoir by Dominique Hunter

My Take On All Fifty States: An Unexpected Quest to See 'Em All, nonfiction by Jim Ford

Geometry of Fire, nonfiction by Paul Warmbier

In the Cloakroom of Proper Musings, a lyric narrative by Kristina Moriconi

Chasing the Dragon's Tail, nonfiction by Craig Fullerton

Pandemic Aftermath: How Coronavirus Changed Global Society, nonfiction by Trond Undheim

Change in 4D, nonfiction by Wendy Wickham

Eyeless Mind, nonfiction by Stephanie Duesing

A Blameless Walk, nonfiction by Charles Hopkins

The Horror of 1888, nonfiction by Betty Plombon

White Snake Diary, nonfiction by Jane P. Perry

From Rags to Rags, essays by Ellie Guzman

ABOUT THE AUTHOR

Patsy Creedy is a writer and a native Californian living in San Francisco with her husband Tim and their nervous dog, Mike. This is her first memoir. She has published poetry and creative nonfiction in several publications. She worked for many years as a labor and delivery nurse before retiring to write fulltime. She is a returning fellow at Dorland Mountain Arts Colony. Pre-pandemic she liked to go Brooklyn as often as possible to see her daughter and her nervous dog, Dave.

CPSIA information can be obtained
at www.ICGtesting.com
Printed in the USA
LVHW111501160421
684723LV00035B/1003